Plant Minds

The idea that plants have minds can sound improbable, but some widely respected contemporary scientists and philosophers find it plausible. It turns out to be rather tricky to vindicate the presumption that plants do not have minds, for doing so requires getting clear about what plants can do and what exactly a mind is.

By connecting the most compelling empirical work on plant behavior with philosophical reflection on the concept of minds, *Plant Minds* aims to help non-experts begin to think clearly about whether plants have minds. Relying on current consensus ideas about minds and plants, Chauncey Maher first presents the best case for thinking that plants do not have minds. Along the way, however, he unearths an idea at the root of that case, the idea that having a mind requires the capacity to represent the world. In the last chapter, he defends a relatively new and insightful theory of mind that rejects that assumption, making room for the possibility that plants do have minds, primarily because they are alive.

Chauncey Maher is Associate Professor at Dickinson College, USA. He is the author of *The Pittsburgh School of Philosophy* (Routledge, 2012).

Routledge Focus on Philosophy

Routledge Focus on Philosophy is an exciting and innovative new series, capturing and disseminating some of the best and most exciting new research in philosophy in short book form. Peer reviewed and at a maximum of fifty thousand words shorter than the typical research monograph, *Routledge Focus on Philosophy* titles are available in both ebook and print on demand format. Tackling big topics in a digestible format the series opens up important philosophical research for a wider audience, and as such is invaluable reading for the scholar, researcher and student seeking to keep their finger on the pulse of the discipline. The series also reflects the growing interdisciplinarity within philosophy and will be of interest to those in related disciplines across the humanities and social sciences.

Forthcoming titles:

The Passing of Temporal Well-Being
Ben Bramble

Intuition as Consciousness Experience
Ole Koksvik

Human Kinds: A Philosophical Defence
Marion Godman

Confucianism and the Philosophy of Well-Being
Richard Kim

The Philosophy and Psychology of Commitment
John Michael

https://www.routledge.com/Routledge-Focus-on-Philosophy/book-series/RFP

Plant Minds
A Philosophical Defense

By Chauncey Maher
Illustrated by Jim Sias

Routledge
Taylor & Francis Group

LONDON AND NEW YORK

First published 2017 by Routledge

2 Park Square, Milton Park, Abingdon, Oxfordshire OX14 4RN
52 Vanderbilt Avenue, New York, NY 10017

Routledge is an imprint of the Taylor & Francis Group, an informa business

First issued in paperback 2019

Library of Congress Cataloging-in-Publication Data
Names: Maher, Chauncey, 1979– author.
Title: Plant minds : a philosophical defense / by Chauncey Maher ;
    illustrated by Jim Sias.
Description: 1 [edition]. | New York : Routledge, 2017. | Series: Routledge
    focus on philosophy ; 1 | Includes bibliographical references and index.
Identifiers: LCCN 2017009378 | ISBN 9781138739192 (hardback :
    alk. paper)
Subjects: LCSH: Plant physiology. | Plants—Psychic aspects.
Classification: LCC QK714.4 .M34 2017 | DDC 581.3/8—dc23
LC record available at https://lccn.loc.gov/2017009378

ISBN: 978-1-138-73919-2 (hbk)
ISBN: 978-0-367-25846-7 (pbk)

Typeset in Times New Roman
by Apex CoVantage, LLC

To my dad, for sharing his love of flowers with me

Contents

Acknowledgments

This book was fun to write, but from time to time I was uneasy. There are a lot of ways I could go wrong. For encouragement and advice early on, I'm grateful to Zed Adams, Colin Allen, Alyssa DeBlasio, Susan Feldman, Peter Godfrey-Smith, Nat Hansen, Bryce Huebner, Matt McAdam, and Crispin Sartwell.

Dickinson College granted me a semester-long sabbatical, which freed me from teaching and administrative work, allowing me to make substantial progress on the manuscript. Jeff Engelhardt was especially indulgent during those many weeks in the fall of 2014, talking with me regularly about philosophy, biology, and style.

Several friends commented helpfully on the penultimate draft. Molly Mullane, who had just graduated after four years of classes with me, has always been perceptive and inquisitive, but still impressed me with her suggestions for how I should be clearer and more engaging. Susan Feldman, Nathaniel Goldberg, and Nat Hansen each showed me different ways I could enrich the philosophical aspects of the book, while not losing my audience. Steve Schmitt gave me the perspective of a biologist, spotting various factual errors, but also helping me think about my audience's assumptions.

Zed Adams commented carefully on the proposal and the penultimate draft of the book, but I am grateful to him for much more than that. Without him, this book wouldn't exist. Over the past fifteen years, we've shared many beers and laughs, talking about lots of things, but especially philosophical theories of the mind. Zed is very good at asking, "But do you really believe that? Is that *true*?" He has helped me appreciate that despite their noble ambition to see things how they really are, philosophers often have distorted conceptions of reality. He pushed me to learn more about nonhuman animals, which eventually grew into a fascination with living things in general. From the start, Zed has been enthusiastic about this book, helping me overcome various doubts about it and myself.

A couple months before I completed the manuscript, it struck me that the book would be better if my friend and colleague Jim Sias did the illustrations. Despite being a busy father and scholar with his own book in progress, he agreed to do it. Dickinson College's Research and Development Committee awarded me a grant to compensate him for his work. Although I knew when I enlisted Jim that he is an excellent artist, as he completed each drawing, I was consistently delighted.

Figures

Tables

1   Do Plants Have Minds?

1. Blithe Confidence

I was certain that plants didn't have minds. So certain, in fact, that I never even considered it. Although they are alive, although they grow, plants just sit there. That doesn't require a mind, or intelligence. On the contrary, such idleness suggests the absence of a mind or intelligence. People use 'vegetable' as a synonym for 'mind-less.' When you veg out, you stop thinking. A person in a persistent vegetative state has "complete unawareness of the self and the environment," and shows "no evidence of . . . responses to . . . stimuli."[1]

Then I learned that some smart, informed people earnestly believe that plants have minds. Writing more than ten years ago in *Nature*, Anthony Trewavas, a fellow of the Royal Society of Edinburgh, plant physiologist, and molecular biologist, said that "the investigation of plant intelligence is becoming a serious scientific endeavor."[2] He was right. There is now a professional society and journal dedicated to exploring the topic.[3]

Watching a time-lapse film of root growth with my six-year-old son, I started to appreciate their point of view. We were astonished at how much the roots looked like worms searching for food. They grow downward, until impeded—perhaps by a pebble—and then they turn, heading downward again after a short distance. If they touch the impediment again, or encounter a new one, they turn again (Figure 1.1). Similarly, although I knew that plants get energy from the sun, in time-lapse video many plants can be seen turning towards the sun; some track the sun's position across the day. On an average 'leafy' tree, you will see that the leaves generally don't overlap, seeming to optimize the amount of leaf surface that is exposed to the sun, thus optimizing access to food.[4]

Plants are impressive in many ways. Bristlecone pines are some of the oldest living things. Methuselah in the White Mountains of California is estimated to be 4,800 years old. Many plants are 'clonal,' producing

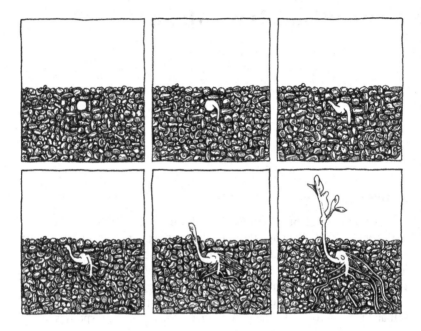

Figure 1.1 Roots and shoots growing

seemingly distinct, but genetically identical individual stems or trunks. Pando, a quaking aspen in Fishlake National Forest in Utah, covers roughly 100 acres, with about 40,000 trunks, and roots estimated to be a shocking 80,000 years old. Banyan trees have adventitious roots that descend from their branches, looking like extra trunks, covering tremendous space. Thimmamma Marrimanu in Andhra Pradesh, India, has a canopy of roughly 4.5 acres, about two city blocks. These numbers are impressive in part because these things are *alive*.

Why was I so sure that plants didn't have minds? It depended, I knew, on what I thought about plants and minds. What can plants do? What is a mind? I didn't know much about plants, but I was so confident that they didn't have minds that I even doubted that learning more about them could convince me otherwise. Thus, I realized that much of my confidence stemmed from what I *assumed* about minds. From my education and research in philosophy, I knew a lot about theories of minds. When I started to reflect on what those theories imply about plants, I expected to be vindicated. I expected to find that the idea of plant minds is very old and was eventually cut down, killed, by more modern theories, even if it wasn't immediately obvious to me which theory struck the lethal blow. To my surprise, that is not what

I found. The idea of plant minds is indeed very old, but it was never killed. Modern theories of minds have actually nourished it—including the theory that currently dominates cognitive science and (broadly Western) philosophizing about the mind.

Uncovering my excessive confidence about plant minds felt, strangely, very good, like noticing for the first time a handsome tree on a path you've traversed for years. It gave me something new and interesting to contemplate: Do plants have minds?

It's worth considering. Whether or not you're open to the possibility that plants have minds, you're probably relying on questionable assumptions about plants, minds, and ourselves, and about life too. Having those assumptions exposed and interrogated can be, I have found, energizing, like breathing fresh air after driving through a recently fertilized cornfield.

In this book, relying on current consensus ideas about minds, I present the best case for thinking that plants do *not* have minds. Along the way, I unearth an idea at the root of that case, the idea that having a mind requires the capacity to represent the world. In the end, I defend a relatively new and insightful theory of mind that rejects that assumption, making room for the possibility that plants do have minds, primarily because they are alive. Throughout, I assume that you, my reader, do not have special knowledge of plants or minds. Thus, I aim to introduce the big ideas to you, making suggestions for further exploration in my footnotes.

In this first chapter, we see that it has been very difficult to figure out what a mind is. Yet doing so is essential for determining whether plants have minds. To help you get started thinking more carefully about whether they do, I will introduce a selection of the most interesting and influential ideas in the history of thinking about minds, ones that will be helpful as we dig deeper. Reflecting on these ideas will also help reveal how I was wrong simply to assume that plants don't have minds.

2. Goal-Directed Order

A truly ancient and compelling idea is that a mind displays a distinctive type of order, order directed at a goal.

Panpsychism is the idea that all things—not just persons or plants, but also puddles, rocks, planets, hair, fire, worms, birds—have a mind or a mental aspect. It may seem outlandish, but some intelligent ancient Greeks found it compelling.[5] When I pause over that fact, one big idea stands out. Nearly everything is orderly.[6] There are patterns or regularities in things. Drop a rock in a puddle; ripples radiate concentrically. Wait a moment; do it again; the same thing happens. Rocks flake and crack in predictable ways when struck. Each day, the sun moves across the sky in the same direction, altering its trajectory incrementally throughout the year. More complicated is the moon's position, its waxing and waning, but there are discernible patterns there too. Plants start small and get bigger; most grow flowers and fruits, then shed them. Although less predictable in various ways, animals, too, are orderly. Dogs chase cats, who chase rats. Flies are drawn to meat and fruit. Like us, the ancient Greeks marveled at the universe, partly because it displays tremendous order.

Now, such order need not imply that each thing has a mind, or that the universe as a whole has a mind, or is made or guided by a mind, but it is tempting to draw that conclusion. The extent and degree of order can seem like they must be produced by intelligence. It is especially tempting to think this in the absence of any plausible alternative.

Aristotle (384–322 B.C.E.) was not a panpsychist, but thought instead that every living thing had psuche (pronounced soo-kay), which is commonly translated as 'soul,' and which is the ancient origin of our root word 'psych-,' as in 'psyche' and 'psychology.'[7] He was an astute observer of organisms; Ernst Mayr, one of the most influential biologists of the twentieth century, thought Aristotle was the most important contributor to biology before Charles Darwin.[8]

That might make it seem as if Aristotle thought every living thing has a mind, but that is not exactly right. What he meant by 'psuche' is not what we often mean by 'mind.' For Aristotle, 'psuche' names the sort of order characteristic of a living thing; it is the way a living thing is directed at a distinctive goal, such as nutrition, or detection of its environment, or understanding of its place in the universe. We, by contrast, use 'mind' for a thing's ability to think and remember. So, we should not hastily equate psuche and mind.

Aristotle thought there were three types of psuche, the highest of which was intellect (what he called 'nous'). The two lower types were nutrition and perception. For him, plants engage in nutrition, the lowest sort of soul, but not the other two; nonhuman animals engage in nutrition and perception, but not intellection; and humans engage in all three. Having a particular type of psuche is to strive toward particular goals, which structure one's activities. Plants grow and seek nourishment, and should be understood and evaluated in terms of whether and how they do so. For instance, an olive tree might not get enough water, and therefore fail to reach its goal of nourishing itself. Nonhuman animals, in addition to seeking nourishment, also perceive their environment, and should be understood and assessed accordingly. For instance, a dog might notice a crevice in its path as it chases a squirrel, turning accordingly. Humans have all three types of psuche, and are distinguished from other organisms by having a rational or intellectual soul, which allows them to deliberate about what to believe (will it rain?) and about what to do (should I visit my friend?).

Thus, in Aristotle, we find the idea that to have 'psuche' is to display a distinctive type of orderliness: orderliness directed toward a goal. Although only humans have the most sophisticated form of it, intellect or reason ('nous'), all organisms display it; all organisms have 'psuche.'

Thus, Aristotle gives us two important ideas about the mind. It is a type of goal-directed order, which is displayed, at different levels, by all living things.

3. Mechanism and Dualism

Thousands of years after Aristotle, in the early seventeenth century in England and Europe, there emerged a new and powerful way to think about the universe, the 'mechanical philosophy.' This spawned the influential idea that a mind is just a mechanism, which spawned the competing and equally influential idea that a mind is a non-material entity. Interestingly, both sever the connection between mind and life; having a mind has nothing to do with being alive.

Mechanical philosophers were guided by two powerful images.[9] They thought the universe is like an enormous clock; it is orderly or regular, and its regularity—its predictability and explicability—is due to the movements of its smaller, constituent parts coming into contact with one another, like the teeth of the gears of a clock (Figure 1.2). A key innovation over older ways of thinking was the hope that we could explain the behavior of the

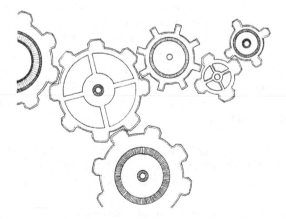

Figure 1.2 Motion work of a clock

whole universe and any of its parts simply in terms of mere matter making contact with more mere matter: teeth on teeth. There was no need to say gears or their teeth have intrinsic affinities or aversions, which seems to anthropomorphize them, to treat them as human. Mere matter does not have affinities or aversions. One tooth just pushes against another, which turns the gear, and one more tooth pushes against another, and so on. Hence our second image: billiard balls colliding. All happenings—the motion of the stars and moon, the gathering of clouds, the growing of a tree, the gait of a horse, the pumping of blood—result from that sort of interaction, bits of matter bumping into each other in regular ways, depending on their speed, trajectory, shape, and rigidity.

The mechanical philosophy supported one important aspect of the broadly Christian worldview that dominated England and Europe at that time. The idea that the universe is like a clock meshes well with the belief that the universe is designed, and thus has a designer, the so-called Argument from Design.[10] Writing many decades after the mechanical philosophers, in his version of the argument, William Paley (1743–1805) relies explicitly on an analogy with a watch:

> In crossing a heath, suppose I pitched my foot against a stone, and were asked how the stone came to be there; I might possibly answer, that, for anything I knew to the contrary, it had lain there forever: nor would it perhaps be very easy to show the absurdity of this answer. But suppose I had found a watch upon the ground, and it should be inquired how the watch happened to be in that place; I should hardly think of the answer I had before given, that for anything I knew, the watch might have always been there. . . . There must have existed, at some time, and at some place or other, an artificer or artificers, who formed [the watch] for the purpose which we find it actually to answer; who comprehended its construction, and designed its use. . . . Every indication of contrivance, every manifestation of design, which existed in the watch, exists in the works of nature; with the difference, on the side of nature, of being greater or more, and that in a degree which exceeds all computation.

Paley says that if you found a watch, you would infer that it has a maker. And since the universe seems at least as sophisticated as a watch, we must also infer that it has a maker, a designer—God. Of course, not everyone has been happy with this analogy, or Paley's argument. What's interesting here is that in revering the clock, mechanical philosophers can still count as good Christians.

But the mechanical philosophy also threatened Christianity. At the heart of Christianity, expressed in the Apostles' Creed and the Nicene Creed, is the belief that we humans are capable of life everlasting, immortality.[11] We can choose how to act, choices for which we deserve reward or punishment, though not necessarily in our lives on earth. To receive what we deserve, we must be made of something that can persist after bodily death. Hence, this something—the soul—must be not just immortal but, in some way, separable from our bodies.

Specifying the exact way in which the soul is separable from the body is not easy, and was contested by many philosophers and theologians after the death of Jesus and into the seventeenth century.[12] For Aristotle, a soul of a body is like a shape of a statue, such as a bronze bust of Aristotle's teacher, Plato. The bronze of which the bust is made is like the body. Aristotle allowed that different hunks of bronze could be given the same shape, or that some particular hunk of bronze could utterly lack the distinctive Plato-shape. But he did not think that the shape could exist by itself; it exists only as the shape of some hunk of matter. Likewise, a soul—the capacity for nutrition, perception, or intellect—cannot exist without a body.

Christian thinkers, such as Augustine (354–430 C.E.) and Thomas Aquinas (1225–1274 C.E.), tended to think differently about it. They allowed that all organisms have souls, of roughly the three types specified by Aristotle, but held also that humans are unique because their soul is not just rational, but immortal and immaterial, capable of existing without the body.[13] Thus, Christians thought that humans and animals are not different in degree, but in kind. A small piece of granite and a large piece of granite differ in degree; they have the same traits, only to different extents. But a piece of granite and a copy of the Bible differ in kind; although they have some of the same traits (weight), one has traits that the other completely lacks. The copy of the Bible has stories. Like Bibles and granite, humans and other organisms differ in kind.[14]

The mechanical philosophy threatened Christianity because it implies that humans do not differ in kind but only in degree from other organisms. Everything is a machine; humans are just more complicated machines. Furthermore, it suggests that if there are souls or minds of any sort, they can be only more matter in motion. As Thomas Hobbes (1588–1679) contended, even reason or intellect is matter in motion.[15] When I think about what to eat for lunch today, debating between a sandwich and a salad, this is ultimately due to the movement and interaction of the matter in me, not an immaterial soul.

Rene Descartes (1596–1650), inventor of the coordinate plane for doing geometry algebraically and a prominent expositor of the mechanical philosophy, resisted the implication that humans are just one machine among others.[16] His solution profoundly affected all subsequent thinking about the mind.

Descartes proposed that there are two fundamentally different substances, body and mind, a view now known as Cartesian Dualism.[17] The defining feature of bodies is that they are spatially extended; they take up space. The behavior of all bodies can and should be understood as the behavior of a machine. For Descartes, this included the reflexive and instinctive behaviors of humans, such as kicking your leg when struck on the knee; they result from pieces of matter exerting force on other pieces of matter. But, Descartes contended, unlike other animals, we humans are not merely our bodies; we are not identical to our bodies; some of our behaviors are not and cannot be understood as merely the operation of a machine. In particular, our speech and thought cannot be explained as the operation of a mere machine. Instead, it must be explained in terms of a second, fundamentally different, immaterial, "non-extended" (non-spatial) substance, a mind.

In correspondence with Descartes, Princess Elisabeth of Bohemia (1618–1680) stressed that his Dualism faces an interaction problem.[18] Your mind affects and is affected by your body: you touch a fleece blanket, and experience a feeling of softness; you decide to say something, and your mouth moves. On Descartes's proposal, however, it is not clear how that could be. For him, by definition, bodies take up space; by definition, minds do not. So, they can never spatially connect. Assuming they do interact, it must be in some as yet unknown way.

In articulating his view, Descartes made the startling claim that all nonhuman organisms are mere machines, "automata."[19] For Descartes, because there are only two sorts of things (two substances), bodies and minds, and because nonhuman organisms are fully explicable as mere bodies, they have no minds (or souls, on the older way of thinking that Descartes was trying to replace). He rebuffed protestations that nonhuman animals seem to have minds: they seem to suffer, play, hide, obey, protect, nurture, and so on.[20] He held instead that their behavior is utterly automatic and predictable, hence no need for reasoning or a mind. Furthermore, whereas humans can speak, which for Descartes implied that they have minds, nonhuman animals clearly cannot speak. He thus held that there was no evidence that nonhuman animals—"brutes"—have minds, and even more so of plants.

Descartes thus radicalized the Christian view that humans are different in kind from other organisms. On the older way of thinking, humans were unique because they have a certain sort of soul, one that is rational, immortal, and separable from the body; other animals and organisms also have souls, just of a lesser, non-rational, sort. Descartes proposed instead that humans are unique simply because they have a mind—which Descartes equated with having a soul—whereas other organisms have no mind (or soul) at all, and are just bodies, machines. Thus, he defended human uniqueness by distinguishing between bodies and minds, and contending that nonhuman organisms are mere bodies without minds (or souls).

A small number of people rejected both Descartes's claims about animals and his Dualism. For instance, in "Man a Machine," writing anonymously, Julian Offray de La Mettrie (1709–1751) contended that humans are machines through and through—not just their bodies, but their minds as well.[21] Their minds are just an aspect, an expression of the machinery that they are. Thus, like Thomas Hobbes before him, La Mettrie was a resolute mechanist. On this way of thinking, nonhuman animals can have minds, since having a mind does not require a second, immaterial substance. In "Man a Plant," La Mettrie went further, emphasizing that because all organisms are just machines, humans are fundamentally similar to plants. He suggested that the mind of humans is just a more sophisticated manifestation of the behavior we see in plants.

La Mettrie's view was well known, but not popular—an object of ridicule, really.[22] When you start with the assumption that the mind is no more than the operation of a machine, you get to the conclusion that humans are not deeply different from plants, which was taken to be patently absurd. Thus, La Mettrie's assumption had to be wrong.

Although many intelligent people rejected Descartes's claims about "brutes"—the claims were, in fact, officially condemned—many also rejected Hobbes's and La Mattrie's claims that creatures with minds are nothing but machines. Instead, they continued to embrace the uniqueness of humans, and accepted Cartesian Dualism.[23]

So, there was a clash between Mechanism and Dualism about the mind.

The mechanical philosophers proposed that everything is mere matter in motion, rigid bodies bumping into one another, including anything that has a mind. Descartes countered: although bodies are mere matter in motion, a mind is a non-material or non-bodily substance; only humans have it; all other organisms are just bodies, mere matter in motion. Despite that significant disagreement, Mechanism and Dualism agreed that Aristotle was wrong, life is not necessary for mind.

Perhaps the most impressive expression of the mechanical philosophy came from Isaac Newton (1643–1726). He proposed that every object in the universe behaves according to three simple "laws," three inviolable regularities that all objects exhibit. First, unless acted upon by some outside

Table 1.1 What is a mind?

	What is a mind?	*Could plants have minds?*
Aristotelianism	Psuche: goal-directed order	Yes
	Nous: intellect or reason	
Mechanism	A type of matter-in-motion	Yes
Cartesian Dualism	A non-bodily entity	No

force, objects at rest tend to stay at rest, and objects in motion tend to stay in motion. Second, the force exerted by an object, such as its weight on earth, is directly proportional to both its mass and its acceleration. (Force = mass × acceleration.) Third, for every action, there is an equal and opposite reaction. Newton's universe was not strictly mechanical, since objects in it can act on one another "at a distance," by gravity, without being in contact with one another. But it was still regarded as essentially mechanical, since it involved only blind hunks of matter pushing and pulling on one another, with astonishing regularity, like a clock.

While the simplicity, scope, and explanatory power of Newton's three laws captivated intelligent people, experts in medicine, anatomy, physiology, and botany nevertheless doubted that living things were mere machines.[24] Though both machines and organisms are orderly, organisms seem to differ because they seem purposive or goal-directed. An embryo, for instance, grows from one cell into an elaborate arrangement of many cells, tissues, organs, and systems of a whole organism, which seeks nourishment and copes with its environment. Cells do not merely divide haphazardly but differentiate into types with distinctive roles within the whole. Larger parts of organisms—such as stems and leaves, or legs and eyes—contribute to the proper operation of the whole organism. Eyes, for instance, are for the whole organism to see as it seeks nourishment and navigates the world. This sort of order—of parts contributing to the goals of wholes—seems utterly different from the way that a hunk of inanimate matter, such as a block of granite, can be said to have parts. You can crack a block of granite into pieces, but not one of those pieces makes a contribution to the whole block in the way that a cell contributes to a tissue, or a tissue to an organ, or an organ to an organism. To people studying these things, it seemed like we cannot understand organisms—humans, animals, plants—by talking only of the aim-less bumping about of matter, but must instead talk of goals or purposes.[25]

4. Evolution by Natural Selection

With the publication of *On the Origin of Species by Means of Natural Selection* in 1859, Charles Darwin (1809–1882) offered a profoundly new way to think about organisms and minds.[26] A mind was an *evolved* trait or set of traits of *organisms*. That idea (temporarily) restored the connection between mind and life.

Darwin appreciated that organisms strike us as peculiarly designed for or adapted to their diverse ways of life. For instance, on the Galapagos Islands, which he visited in 1835, he found a wide variety of finches, each with a distinctive beak. Some have large beaks; others have curved beaks;

still others have long, narrow beaks (Figure 1.3). Thanks to the painstaking research more than a century later by Peter and Rosemary Grant, it is clear that each of these beaks is especially well suited for eating only certain types of foods.[27] The beak of, say, the Large Ground Finch, is excellent for cracking large, hard seeds, common in its habitat. How could that be? Why do the Large Ground Finches have beaks that fit their needs and habitat so well? Furthermore, why are other finches with different beaks well suited for other foods? It is as if the finches and their beaks have been designed precisely for their habitat.

Darwin proposed that all organisms result from a process that is similar to the breeding of pigeons by humans, which was a popular hobby in Darwin's time. Breeders would select a trait that they wanted to enhance, such as a tall plume, and then would encourage pigeons with it to mate, hoping for offspring that had a more pronounced form of that trait, a taller plume. According to Darwin, a similar process of selection happens in nature— "natural selection"—but without a person or breeder to initiate and guide the process. Instead, organisms happen to interact with one another and their environments in various ways, some surviving longer and reproducing more or more effectively than others. As this process is repeated over many generations and years, the overall effect is like the effect of breeding, except

Figure 1.3 Darwin's finches

here traits that better fit the circumstances tend to be passed on, while others do not. For instance, finches with beaks that are better at cracking available seeds will tend to live longer and have a better chance at reproducing than finches that are otherwise similar but lack that sort of beak. Thus, later generations of finches come to have beaks that suit available seeds. It is as if they were "designed" or "selected" for those seeds, even though there was no designer or selector.[28]

Darwin was widely seen as attacking Christianity. He showed how it could seem as if organisms were designed even if they were not designed at all, thus undermining the Argument from Design. He also gave us an alternative to the dominant, Christian way of thinking about the diversity of living things, according to which each species—paramecia, earthworms, honeybees, daffodils, cows, orangutans, and humans—had been deliberately and individually created by God several thousand years ago, and has remained that way. On that way of thinking, the similarity between many species, such as their bilaterally symmetrical bodies, reflects God's ideas about which structures are best. By contrast, Darwin proposed that all organisms descend from a single common ancestor with myriad, gradually accumulated, modifications—"descent with modification." Like the way that organisms are peculiarly adapted to their life circumstances, the diversity of life results from natural selection. Thus, for Darwin, all organisms are not simply similar—having, for instance, similar bodies—as are a layer cake and an office building, but are in fact ancestrally related, like very distant cousins. Humans are literally relatives of all other organisms. That suggests that humans cannot differ in kind from other organisms, as Christianity insists.

Darwin also suggested we must give up Dualism.[29] At the time, more than two centuries after Descartes's death in 1650, many intelligent people still espoused some form of it. They held that the mind was a special sort of entity or substance that was either identical to or an aspect of an immaterial soul; it was not a merely bodily or material thing or process; humans have it, but the vast majority of other organisms do not. Darwin's way of thinking challenged each of those ideas. Since all traits and aptitudes of organisms arise from natural selection of material bodies, the mind cannot be an immaterial entity, but is at most a suite of aptitudes of fully material things. Furthermore, since all organisms are related by descent with modification, the mind cannot be utterly without precedent in nonhuman organisms. In *The Descent of Man*, Darwin wrote, "the difference in mind between man and the higher animals, great as it is, certainly is one of degree and not of kind."[30] For him, humans and other animals are not only biologically similar, but also psychologically similar. In *The Power of Movement in Plants*,

Table 1.2 What is a mind?

	What is a mind?	Could plants have minds?
Aristotelianism	Psuche: goal-directed order Nous: intellect or reason	Yes
Mechanism	A type of matter-in-motion	Yes
Cartesian Dualism	A non-bodily entity	No
Darwinism	A suite of abilities resulting from evolution by natural selection	Yes

Darwin extended this way of thinking: "it is impossible not to be struck with the resemblance between the . . . movements of plants and many of the actions performed unconsciously by the lower animals."[31] He hypothesized that at the apices of their stems and roots, plants have sense organs roughly analogous to eyes.[32]

5. Behaviorism

Roughly fifty years after Darwin, John Watson (1878–1958) articulated a shockingly simple idea about minds: they are nothing more than behavioral dispositions.

Watson's idea grew out of a series of fascinating developments in physiology, animal studies, and psychology. Before Watson, Conwy Lloyd Morgan (1852–1936) aimed to move the study of minds beyond mere anecdote, hoping to make the proper study of animal behavior much more systematic and controlled.[33] It was not enough simply to see one occasion on which a dog unlatches a gate with its muzzle, and conclude that it knows how latches or gates work. One had at least to watch the dog at the gate on several occasions. Ideally, one could see the dog's first and subsequent encounters with the gate, tracking what the dog does and does not do. And even then, one must be careful about what exactly one concludes about what the dog knows or understands. Morgan was particularly worried that anecdotes tended to be embarrassingly anthropomorphic, treating animals as if they were humans. He stressed that interpretations of animal behavior must be cautious about attributing mental abilities to animals. He proposed that we must never say an animal's behavior involves a "higher psychological process"—such as deliberation—if a "lower" one—such as trial-and-error learning—would fit the behavior just as well. We should not say that the dog understands how latches work, if the dog's behavior can be explained just as well by saying that the dog simply has learned a habit, a tendency to move its body parts in a certain order. Eventually labeled "Morgan's Canon," this dictum about how to interpret animal behavior became and has remained very influential in comparative psychology.[34]

Edward Thorndike (1874–1949) built on Morgan's ideas about the dog at the gate, devising a puzzle box with which to test cats and dogs.[35] He placed individual animals in a box with a simple latch holding the door shut. How long would it take to escape? Do animals escape more quickly when given a second, third, or fourth chance? Thorndike tallied his answers, and was thus able to chart their learning curves—the speed with which they perform a task relative to the number of attempts at that task. In general, he found that with additional trials, animals escaped faster. Whereas Morgan had thought that in this sort of process, animals developed connections between ideas, between an idea of an action and an idea of its consequence, Thorndike proposed instead that animals were simply forming a connection between a stimulus and a "motor impulse."[36] There was no connection between ideas. To get out of the box, cats and dogs need not do any thinking at all. Thorndike further proposed that such learning obeyed a fairly simple law, his Law of Effect.[37] Responses to a situation that please the animal will tend to be repeated in that situation; responses that don't please the animal well tend not to be repeated. Although Thorndike initially did not think his ideas applied to humans, eventually he came to think that they did, that human behavior is not fundamentally different from that of other animals; it obeys the same laws.

At the time, although psychology was considered primarily the study of the *human* mind, Morgan and Thorndike saw their studies of animals as connected to psychology. For most psychologists, the most appropriate way to study the human mind was by introspection, by carefully observing and recording one's own mental goings on in different situations. What happens when I look at a tree? What passes through my mind as I hammer a nail into a board? When I deliberate about which road to take, what transpires? For Morgan and Thorndike, since no one could introspect the mind of a nonhuman animal, to observe what it is or is not conscious of, or even whether it is conscious at all, the next best thing was to study their behavior, and then use what we know from human introspection to formulate hypotheses about what's happening in the minds of animals. But these hypotheses should be cautious—abiding by Morgan's Canon—and are not as important as the experiments on animal behavior, which revealed what animals could actually be seen to do. Thus, Morgan and Thorndike inaugurated a behavior-centered approach to the study of animal minds that lasted for decades.

Around this time, there was also great interest in the behavior of other organisms, especially plants and protozoa (single-celled organisms, such as paramecia).[38] Researchers faced questions related to those faced by Morgan, Thorndike, and others studying animals. Did the movement of plants, such as the way they bend toward a light source, require sense organs? Or was it merely mechanical, the result of mere matter exerting pressure on mere matter? Decades earlier, in 1848, Gustav Fechner had articulated and defended the idea that plants have a soul—an animating life force—and were not mere machines. By the time Darwin and his son Francis (1848–1925) published their research on plant movements in 1880, the dominant view was that plants were wholly material things, but were nevertheless "sensitive" to their environment; they could detect changes in their environment and respond appropriately—for instance, by turning towards the sun. (Remember, Aristotle had denied that plants perceive.) Darwin contended that this sensitivity required something analogous to the sense organs of animals. Julius von Sachs and Julius von Wiesner, who were respected botanical experimenters, disagreed. Jacques Loeb went further, arguing that plant sensitivity could be understood in wholly mechanical terms; there was no need to appeal to an immaterial soul, a mind, sense organs, or goal-directedness; plants turn this way or that because their material parts are blindly pushed in this way or that way by other material things. Yet in the same year that Loeb's book appeared, 1888, Alfred Binet proposed that even "micro-organisms" have a "psychic life." And in 1908, in his Presidential Address to the British Association for the Advancement of Science, Francis Darwin, who had become a distinguished botanist, made a case for consciousness in plants, claiming that "we must believe that in plants there exists a faint copy of what we know as consciousness in ourselves."[39]

Since researchers of animal behavior like Morgan and Thorndike were very cautious—nearly skeptical—about appeals to the mind to explain animal behavior, psychologists questioned whether such animal studies really belonged to psychology. The intense focus on experiments on behavior and movement made such work seem more like *physi*ology. For John Watson, these doubts had special force. He was a careful researcher of rat behavior, but also a professor in the psychology department at Johns Hopkins University, and the editor of the *Psychological Review*, the discipline's premier journal.[40]

Watson's defense of his type of work was a bold "manifesto," articulating a new vision for psychology.[41] In "Psychology as the Behaviorist Views It" published in 1913, Watson contended that the only proper object of study for psychology was behavior. This was not simply because studying behavior was the best way to get at the mind, better than introspection. Rather, it was because there was simply no more to the mind than habits of behavior, patterns of response to stimuli. Dualism was definitely false. Furthermore, this was true not only of "brutes," but humans, too. Watson wrote:

Psychology as the behaviorist views it is a purely objective experimental branch of natural science. Its theoretical goal is the prediction and control of behavior. Introspection forms no essential part of its methods, nor is the scientific value of its data dependent upon the readiness with which they lend themselves to interpretation in terms of consciousness. The behaviorist, in his efforts to get a unitary scheme of animal response, recognizes no dividing line between man and brute. The behavior of man, with all of its refinement and complexity, forms only part of the behaviorist's total scheme of investigation.[42]

If Watson was right, then it was extremely plausible that plants might have minds. For if having a mind was simply a matter of behavior, of patterns of responding to stimuli, which plants were already then recognized to do, then plants could have minds.

But was Watson right?

Psychologists have tended to distinguish different varieties of behaviorism, different ideas that can plausibly be labeled 'behaviorism.'[43] Watson is typically regarded as a *Radical* Behaviorist, aiming to explain a creature's behavior solely by appeal to patterns of stimulus and response, the creature's learning history, eschewing entirely appeals to the creature's mind or consciousness, such as what it believes, notices, or remembers. This is different and stronger than *Methodological* Behaviorism, according to which the best way to *study* 'the mind' is to study behavior. When explaining a creature's behavior, a Methodological Behaviorist can happily appeal to more than that creature's learning history, but a Radical Behaviorist cannot. Whereas Radical Behaviorism is a thesis about how to explain behavior, and Methodological Behaviorism is a thesis about how to study behavior, *Analytical* or Logical Behaviorism is a thesis about the meaning of "mental terms," such as 'believe,' 'notice,' and 'remember'. It holds such terms are or should be *defined* in terms of behavior. For instance, 'believe' should be defined in terms of dispositions to behave some way or other. If you believe X, then when a friend happens to say "X is false," you will likely say "You're mistaken." Analytical Behaviorism, in effect, claims that minds (mental states) are dispositions to behave.[44]

After Watson's initial article and subsequent textbook articulating his vision, many psychologists embraced only Methodological Behaviorism. For them, the mind was more than the sum of an organism's habits, but introspection was not adequately scientific; there was no good way to test and verify introspective reports; no good way to experiment on phenomena available only through introspection; the best way to study the mind was to study behavior.

Some psychologists, however, especially B.F. Skinner (1904–1990), embraced the more contentious position of Radical Behaviorism.[45] A dog does not remember how to open the gate; instead, by reinforcement of

Table 1.3 What is a mind?

	What is a mind?	Could plants have minds?
Aristotelianism	Psuche: goal-directed order	Yes
	Nous: intellect or reason	
Mechanism	A type of matter-in-motion	Yes
Cartesian Dualism	A non-bodily entity	No
Darwinism	A suite of abilities resulting from evolution by natural selection	Yes
Behaviorism	Dispositions to behave, which can be gained and lost through habituation	Yes

past movements of its neck, head, and muzzle in relation to the gate, it has acquired a habit of moving its neck, head, and muzzle so as to open the gate. No remembering required. Skinner used the strategy for human beings.

Radical Behaviorism can seem crazy. Obviously, we have minds! Nothing could be easier for each of us to notice than our own thoughts. Skinner, of course, was perfectly aware that we confidently claim to have minds. For him, however, such talk is simply one important behavioral datum among others that requires explanation. We talk about our minds, our thoughts and feelings, but that does not by itself imply that they are real items inside of us. Skinner held that such talk is to be explained by our admittedly complicated learning histories. To this, many have been tempted to say maybe so, but that does not imply that one's mind is no more than the sum of one's habits, one's dispositions to behave. Granted, there are crucial connections between dispositions to behave and the mind, but that does not make them one and the same. My thought that Skinner was a tenacious theorist differs from my reporting that thought aloud to you, or a disposition to report it at all.

Apart from these arguments seemingly rooted in "common sense," Radical Behaviorism faced several important experimental challenges.[46] Noam Chomsky articulated probably the most famous problem for a Radical Behaviorist approach to human behavior. A typical utterance of a human being cannot be explained simply by appeal to his or her learning history.[47] Chomsky stressed that even a child has a mastery of grammar that goes beyond his or her learning history; the child knows more than he or she has been taught, or could have learned by mere observation. But Radical Behaviorism also had difficulty dealing with the behavior of nonhuman animals. For instance, a rat familiar with a maze is able to find a shortcut through that maze even though the rat has never before traversed or encountered that shortcut. Its learning history, thus, seems unable to account for its behavior. Rather, the rat seems to be relying on a thought about the maze, an inner, "cognitive map." (More on this later.)

Although aspects of Radical Behaviorism continue to influence contemporary psychological research in humans and animals, it is rejected by most contemporary psychologists.

6. Computationalism

We come now to the final two ideas about minds that I want to introduce you to in this chapter. The first is the Identity Theory of Mind, the idea that the mind is simply the brain and nervous system. The second is the Computational Theory of Mind, the idea that the mind is a computer. Although every idea I have presented continues to be influential, these final two ideas are especially so. The Computational Theory, in particular, is the heart of contemporary psychology. Accordingly, it will have a special place in the rest of our inquiry.

One attractive alternative to behaviorism is the idea that the mind is nothing more than the brain and nervous system: mental states and processes, such as seeing, remembering, and intending, are simply states and processes of the brain and nervous system. Among philosophers, this is known as the Identity Theory of Mind, for it proposes that the mind is not an immaterial substance or an effect of bodily activity, but literally *identical* to the activity of the brain and nervous system.[48] It was latent in some neurology and psychiatry of the late nineteenth and early twentieth centuries, but was explicitly articulated and defended by several philosophers in the 1950s: U.T. Place, J.J.C. Smart, and Herbert Feigl.[49] According to the Identity Theory, Radical Behaviorism mistakenly looks only at the training and behavioral dispositions of whole humans and animals, rather than the anatomical and physiological specifics of those creatures.

The Identity Theory was and remains compelling to a wide range of intelligent people. However, from its earliest days, many have found it questionable, and not just because they are convinced we have an immaterial soul. Many philosophers have had a hard time making good sense of the claim that a mental state just is a state of the brain or nervous system. Crucially, the Identity Theory does *not* claim merely that a mental state is an *effect* of the brain and nervous system. Rather, it claims that they are *identical*, as when we say that water is identical to H_2O. They are one and the very same thing, labeled in two different ways, understood in different ways, learned at different times, with varying degrees of effort. To be sad, mad, or glad is simply for one's brain and nervous system to be in a certain state. An implication is that when properly done, psychology will become neurology.

In one version of the theory, concepts pertaining to the mind, such as that of perception, belief, deliberation, and intention, are only very crude tools for thinking about human and animal behavior; good science should show us how to replace them, as when doctors gave up thinking about health in terms of the four humors (blood, phlegm, black bile, and green bile).[50]

Maybe the most problematic implication of the Identity Theory is that things without brains or nervous systems cannot count as having minds. A robot couldn't have one; nor could any alien life form that happened to lack a brain and nervous system, no matter how sophisticated it might be. In defense of the Identity Theory, it might be tempting to say that so long as an anatomical structure operates like the brain and nervous system, it can count as having a mind. Yet that reply starts drifting away from the Theory. Its distinctive claim is that the mind is identical to the brain and nervous system, not just any anatomical structure that exhibits similar processes.[51] This difficulty points toward the Computational Theory of Mind.

That Theory is the heart of contemporary psychology. It grew largely out of the doubts about behaviorism.[52] As Margaret Boden relates in her monumental, two-volume history of cognitive science, in the 1940s, information theory and computers offered models for articulating a new vision of the mind, one that was not a mere return to the introspective methods of old, but gave instead a rigorous way to think about the "inner" processes that behaviorism pushes aside (and which the Identity Theory proposes are nothing but processes in the nervous system).[53] According to the Computational Theory, the mind is like a computer: it receives input, manipulates it, and produces some output. Consider a simple electronic calculator. You punch some keys in a certain order: 5, 7, +, 6, 8, =. An instant later, the screen shows 125. In that very brief instant, rule-governed processes have occurred inside the device that yield the number on the screen. The pressing of the keys is like experience; the inner, intermediate processes are like thinking or reasoning; the output number is like behavior. A calculator is, of course, only a very simple computer; a mind is certainly more complex than that. But the basic analogy is what mattered. The mind is more-or-less like a computer. Mental states are more or less like states or processes that mediate between input and output. In these terms, Radical Behaviorism seems to have recognized only input and output, ignoring the states that mediate between them. The Identity Theory misses the computational and informational character of psychological processes.

This picture of the mind was captured in 1960, in another "manifesto," *Plans and the Structure of Behavior* by George Miller, Eugene Galanter, and Karl Pribram. Although the specifics of their vision are now generally thought to be flawed, in contemporary cognitive science and philosophy of mind, the basic view of the mind as a computer has become mainstream.[54]

On the face of it, the Computational Theory of Mind appears to kill the idea that plants have minds, for plants don't seem to be computers. But that appearance might be deceptive. If computation is simply information processing, then plants might have minds.[55] Information processing is the systematic transformation of one informational state into another. An informational state is one that varies or correlates with another, thus carrying information about it. Tree rings, for instance, are informational states because they correlate with the age of the tree; they carry information about the age of the tree. Plants seem like they are information processors because they seem to convert informational states into other informational states. When a piece of canary grass bends toward a light source, the initial informational state is the state of the photoreceptors that vary with the presence of light; there are several intervening such states; and the 'final' informational state is the orientation of the apex towards that light source (Figure 1.4). That is just one example, but there are others, which we will consider in due course.[56]

Figure 1.4 Canary grass (*Phalaris canariensis*)

Table 1.4 What is a mind?

	What is a mind?	*Could plants have minds?*
Aristotelianism	Psuche: goal-directed order Nous: intellect or reason	Yes
Mechanism	A type of matter-in-motion	Yes
Cartesian Dualism	A non-bodily entity	No (?)
Darwinism	A suite of abilities resulting from evolution by natural selection	Yes
Behaviorism	Dispositions to behave, which can be gained and lost through habituation	Yes
Identity Theory	The (human?) nervous system	No
Computationalism	A computer	Yes

The last table in this chapter (Table 1.4) shows that some of the most influential ideas about minds leave open the possibility that plants have them. Only two—the Identity Theory and Cartesian Dualism—appear to rule it out. And even that is questionable. Strictly speaking, Cartesian Dualism does not say that plants cannot have minds. Rather, it says only that a mind is a non-bodily, non-extended substance. Like humans, plants could be made of it. Descartes, however, contended further that the main mark of being so made was the capacity for speech. (Indeed, he seems to have taken for granted that only humans have minds, and used that to substantiate the claim that speech is the mark of the mind.) And plants don't seem able to speak. So, it is only in conjunction with a further assumption about minds that even Cartesian Dualism rules out the possibility that plants have minds.

Whereas the mechanical philosophy and Radical Behaviorism might seem to nourish the idea of plant minds only by relying on implausible conceptions of minds, things look different with the Computational Theory of Mind. Although it faces important challenges, it is the dominant view in cognitive science and philosophy of mind.[57] We must take it seriously.

7. The Plan

I've introduced several important ideas about the mind, what it is, and some of the implications for plant minds. You don't need to have mastered these ideas; you will encounter each again later, in subsequent chapters. I do hope, however, that you have started thinking more carefully about the mind, excavating some of your own assumptions. And I hope you appreciate the need to dig deeper.

In anticipation of the end of our inquiry, let me highlight one significant lesson of our brief tour through history: life has posed a challenge for thinking about the mind. For instance, if purposiveness requires a mind, then all living things have minds, since all living things are purposive. Most theorists, however, think that only humans and some animals have minds. Thus, they will want to reject that little bit of reasoning. (Most likely, they would try to deny that purposiveness requires having a mind.) The challenge is to draw a line in a reasonable way, between living things that have minds and those that don't. These theorists need to explain what a mind is in a way that does not blithely assimilate being alive to being a mere machine or a mere aggregate of matter.

I have structured the rest of our inquiry around a common assumption guiding past and current thinking about the mind: it has several facets, or involves several interconnected abilities, primarily perception, feeling, memory, and action. Roughly, anything with a mind perceives things, feels things, remembers things, and acts on the basis of what it perceives, feels, and remembers. Each chapter focuses on one of these facets, asking two basic questions: (1) What is it? and (2) Do plants have it? Specifically, we shall consider:

Do plants perceive?
Do they feel? Are they conscious?
Do plants remember?
Do they act?

We will find that if we accept currently dominant ideas about these facets of mind, we must conclude that plants don't have minds. However, I will contend that we need not accept those dominant ideas. There is instead a relatively new, minority view of the mind that supports thinking that plants do have minds, or at least, proto-minds. In the final chapter, I will argue that this view is more plausible than it might seem at first, and that there is good reason to think that plants—indeed all living things—have minds.

Many intriguing and challenging topics lie ahead, so allow me to offer you some good advice about how to think about our endeavor. Virtually unknown outside the academy, but very highly regarded among contemporary philosophers, Wilfrid Sellars (1908–1987) once wrote:

> The aim of philosophy, abstractly formulated, is to understand how things in the broadest possible sense of the term hang together in the broadest possible sense of the term. Under 'things in the broadest

possible sense' I include such radically different items as not only 'cabbages and kings', but also numbers and duties, possibilities and finger snaps, aesthetic experience and death. To achieve success in philosophy would be, to use a contemporary turn of phrase, to 'know one's way around' with respect to all these things, not in that unreflective way in which the centipede of the story knew its way around before it faced the question, 'how do I walk?', but in that reflective way which means that no intellectual holds are barred.[58]

Sellars's thought guides me in this book. I have tried to understand how ideas from philosophy, botany, and cognitive science hang together. Nearly all of these ideas are perfectly familiar to philosophers, botanists, *or* cognitive scientists, but only a few of them are familiar to philosophers, botanists, *and* cognitive scientists.[59] In general, I have assumed that most of these ideas are not familiar to you, my reader, and that you are simply willing to inquire with no intellectual holds barred.

Notes

1 (Multi-Society Task Force on PVS, 1994). For more recent discussion, see (Jennett, 2005).
2 (Trewavas, 2002, p. 841).
3 See, for instance, (Trewavas, 2004), (Brenner, Stahlberg, Mancuso, Baluška, & Volkenburgh, 2007), and (Calvo & Keijzer, 2011).
4 For a wonderful collection of time-lapse videos of such movements, go to Plants-in-Motion online, run by Roger Hangarter of the Department of Biology at Indiana University.
5 See, for instance, (Skrbina, 2005).
6 This is not the dominant argument for panpsychism. Rather, the dominant argument begins from a dilemma: either everything has a mind, or things with minds emerged from things without minds. The next step contends that it is not possible for things with minds to emerge from things without minds. Thus, so the argument goes, everything has a mind. See, for instance, (Seager & Allen-Hermanson, 2010).
7 For his main remarks on the soul, see (Aristotle, 1984/1995). For helpful overviews of Aristotle's thinking about 'psuche,' see (Shields, 2010) and (Everson, 1995).
8 (Mayr, 1982, p. 87).
9 In addition to Thomas Hobbes and Rene Descartes, other mechanical philosophers included Robert Boyle (MacIntosh & Anstey, 2014), and Pierre Gassendi (Fisher, 2013).
10 A version of the argument appears in Aquinas's *Summa Theologica*. See the "fifth way" of proving the existence of god, under Question 2, Article 3, of the First Part. For an overview of the Argument from Design, see (Himma, 2009).
11 See, for instance, (Keating, 1908).
12 See, for instance, (King, 2012) and (Pasnau, 2012).
13 See, for instance, (McInerny & O'Callaghan, 2014) and (Mendelson, 2010).

14 See, for instance, (Thomas, 1996).
15 (Hobbes, 1651/1982).
16 See, for instance, (Descartes, 1637/1999), (Fuchs, 2001), and (Hatfield, 2014).
17 See, for instance, the sixth meditation in (Descartes, 1641/1996).
18 (Elisabeth & Descartes, 2007).
19 See, for instance, part V of (Descartes, 1637/1999).
20 See, for instance, his letter to the Marquess of Newcastle, of 23 November 1646, and his letter to Henry More, of 5 February 1649, printed in (Descartes, 1970).
21 (de La Mettrie, 1748/1994).
22 See, for instance, (Leiber, 1748/1994).
23 See (Gaukroger, 1995). In 1663, the Catholic Church banned *Meditations*. In 1706, the Jesuits condemned Descartes's claim that animals lacked souls.
24 See, for instance, (Kitcher, 1981), (Grene & Depew, 2004), (Mayr, 1982), and (Bechtel & Richardson, 1998).
25 A more thorough discussion of this issue would address the work of Immanuel Kant (1724–1804), who argued that although all organisms, including humans, are indeed mechanisms, we humans cannot help conceiving of organisms as more than that, as goal-directed. See, for instance, (Kant, 1790/2000), (Rohlf, 2010), (Ginsborg, 2013) (Brigandt & Love, 2012), and (Weber & Varela, 2002).
26 (Boakes, 1984).
27 (Weiner, 1994).
28 See, for instance, (Brandon, 2008) and (Futuyma, 2005).
29 (Boakes, 1984).
30 (Darwin, C., 1882, p. 126).
31 (Darwin & Darwin, 1880, p. 571); cited by Francis Darwin in his Presidential Address to the British Association for the Advancement of Science (Darwin, F., 1908, p. 354).
32 (Whippo & Hangarter, 2009).
33 (Boakes, 1984, pp. 32–44).
34 See, for instance, (Allen & Bekoff, 1999) and (Shettleworth, 2009).
35 (Boakes, 1984, pp. 68–78).
36 (Boakes, 1984, p. 71).
37 (Thorndike, 1911, p. 244). Thorndike initially reported his ideas in (Thorndike, 1898). As Boakes documents, Thorndike's Law was anticipated by Spencer, Bain, and Morgan (Boakes, 1984, p. 74).
38 (Boakes, 1984, pp. 137–143). See also (Whippo & Hangarter, 2009).
39 (Darwin, F., 1908, p. 362).
40 (Boakes, 1984, pp. 137–143).
41 (Boakes, 1984, pp. 148, 167).
42 (Watson, 1913, p. 158).
43 For an illuminating, short history of the term 'radical behaviorism,' see (Schneider & Morris, 1987).
44 For this way of defining the various behaviorisms, see (Rey, 1997).
45 (Skinner, 1945), (Skinner, 1953), and (Skinner, 1963).
46 These criticisms are nicely chronicled in (Rey, 1997).
47 (Chomsky, 1957).
48 See, for instance, (Smart, 2007).
49 (Place, 1956), (Feigl, 1958), and (Smart, 1959).
50 This is called "eliminative materialism" (Ramsey, 2013). It is most commonly associated with Patricia and Paul Churchland.

51 A more plausible and more widely endorsed version of the Identity Theory acknowledges this shortcoming, and holds instead that each mental state is identical to *some physical state or other*. It gives up the claim that for each *type* of mental state, there is precisely one type of physical state with which it is identical. The difference is subtle but significant. It is comparable to the difference between claiming that all chess pieces are made of wood and claiming that all chess pieces are made of some physical material or other.

52 See, for instance, (Sternberg, 2008) and (Boden, 2006).

53 (Boden, 2006).

54 See, for instance, (Piccinini, 2009) and (Milkowski, 2013).

55 (Calvo, 2007) and (Calvo & Keijzer, 2011).

56 If, instead, computation is something like speaking an inner language, then plants might not be computers. (Fodor, 1975) is the locus classicus for the idea of a "language of thought." However, versions of the idea were anticipated by Plato and Thomas Aquinas.

57 In later chapters, I discuss some of these challenges. Representative work includes: (Dreyfus, 1992/1972), (Haugeland, 1978), (van Gelder, 1995), (Clark, 1997), and especially (Thompson, 2007).

58 (Sellars, 1963, p. 1). Until Nat Hansen asked me to look into it, I did not know that the story to which Sellars refers is, almost surely, "The Centipede's Dilemma," a poem attributed to Katherine Craster (1841–1874). It reads:

A centipede was happy—quite!
Until a toad in fun
Said, "Pray, which leg moves after which?"
This raised her doubts to such a pitch,
She fell exhausted in the ditch
Not knowing how to run.

59 In general, the topic of plant minds or plant intelligence has not been discussed much by contemporary philosophers. Important exceptions are (Dretske, 1999), (Calvo, 2007), (Calvo & Keijzer, 2011), (Hall, 2011), and (Marder, 2013).

Works Cited

Allen, C., & Bekoff, M. (1999). *Species of Mind*. Cambridge, MA: MIT Press.

Aristotle. (1984/1995). On the Soul. In Aristotle & J. Barnes (Ed.), *The Complete Works of Aristotle*. Princeton, NJ: Princeton University Press.

Bechtel, W., & Richardson, R. (1998). Vitalism. In E. Craig (Ed.), *Routledge Encyclopedia of Philosophy*. New York: Routledge.

Boakes, R. (1984). *From Darwin to Behaviourism*. New York: Cambridge University Press.

Boden, M. (2006). *Mind as Machine: A History of Cognitive Science* (Vol. 1). New York: Clarendon.

Brandon, R. (2008, June 7). *Natural Selection*. Retrieved from Stanford Encyclopedia of Philosophy: http://plato.stanford.edu/entries/natural-selection/

Brenner, E., Stahlberg, R., Mancuso, S., Baluška, F., & Volkenburgh, E. V. (2007). Response to Alpi et al.: Plant Neurobiology: The Gain Is More Than the Name. *Trends in Plant Science, 12*(6), 231–233.

Brigandt, I., & Love, A. (2012, April 30). *Reductionism in Biology*. Retrieved from Stanford Encyclopedia of Philosophy: http://plato.stanford.edu/entries/reduction-biology/

Calvo, P. (2007). The Quest for Cognition in Plant Biology. *Plant Signaling & Behavior*, *2*(4), 208–211.

Calvo, P., & Keijzer, F. (2011). Plants: Adaptive Behavior, Root-Brains, and Minimal Cognition. *Adaptive Behavior*, *19*(3), 155–171.

Chomsky, N. (1957). A Review of B. F. Skinner's Verbal Behavior. *Language*, *35*(1), 26–58.

Clark, A. (1997). *Being There: Putting Brain, Body and World Together Again*. Cambridge, MA: MIT Press.

Darwin, C. (1882). *The Descent of Man* (2nd ed.). London: John Murray.

Darwin, C., & Darwin, F. (1880). *The Power of Movement of Plants*. London: John Murray.

Darwin, F. (1908). The Address of the President of the British Association for the Advancement of Science, I. *Science*, *28*(719), 353–362.

de La Mettrie, J. O. (1748/1994). *Man a Machine and Man a Plant* (R. A. Watson & M. Rybalka, Trans.). Indianapolis, IN: Hackett.

Descartes, R. (1637/1999). *Discourse on the Method* (D. A. Cress, Trans.). Indianapolis, IN: Hackett.

Descartes, R. (1641/1996). *Meditations on First Philosophy* (J. Cottingham, Trans.). New York: Cambridge University Press.

Descartes, R. (1970). *Descartes: Philosophical Letters* (A. Kenny, Ed.). Minneapolis, MN: University of Minnesota.

Dretske, F. (1999). Machines, Plants, and Animals. *Erkenntnis*, *51*(1), 19–31.

Dreyfus, H. (1972/1992). *What Computers (Still) Can't Do* (2nd ed.). Cambridge, MA: MIT Press.

Elisabeth, P. O., & Descartes, R. (2007). *The Correspondence Between Princess Elisabeth of Bohemia and René Descartes* (L. Shapiro, Ed., & L. Shapiro, Trans.). Chicago: University of Chicago Press.

Everson, S. (1995). Psychology. In J. Barnes (Ed.), *The Cambridge Companion to Aristotle* (pp. 168–194). New York: Cambridge University Press.

Feigl, H. (1958). The 'Mental' and the 'Physical'. In H. Feigl, M. Scriven, & G. Maxwell (Eds.), *Minnesota Studies in the Philosophy of Science* (Vol. II, pp. 370–497). Minneapolis: University of Minnesota.

Fisher, S. (2013, November 18). *Pierre Gassendi*. Retrieved from Stanford Encyclopedia of Philosophy: http://plato.stanford.edu/entries/gassendi/

Fodor, J. (1975). *The Language of Thought*. New York: Crowell.

Fuchs, T. (2001). *The Mechanization of the Heart: Harvey & Descartes* (M. Grene, Trans.). Rochester, NY: University of Rochester Press.

Futuyma, D. (2005). *Evolution*. Sunderland, MA: Sinauer Assoc.

Gaukroger, S. (1995). *Descartes: An Intellectual Biography*. New York: Clarendon.

Ginsborg, H. (2013, February 13). *Kant's Aesthetics and Teleology*. Retrieved from Stanford Encyclopedia of Philosophy: http://plato.stanford.edu/entries/kant-aesthetics/

Grene, M., & Depew, D. (2004). *The Philosophy of Biology: An Episodic History*. New York: Cambridge University Press.

Hall, M. (2011). *Plants as Persons*. New York: SUNY.

Hatfield, G. (2014, January 16). *Rene Descartes*. Retrieved from Stanford Encyclopedia of Philosophy: http://plato.stanford.edu/entries/descartes/

Haugeland, J. (1978). The Nature and Plausibility of Cognitivism. *Behavioral and Brain Sciences, 1*(2), 215–226.

Himma, K. (2009). *Design Arguments for the Existence of God*. Retrieved from Internet Encyclopedia of Philosophy: www.iep.utm.edu/design/

Hobbes, T. (1651/1982). *Leviathan*. New York: Penguin.

Jennett, B. (2005). Thirty Years of the Vegetative State: Clinical, Ethical and Legal Problems. *Progress in Brain Research, 150*, 537–543.

Kant, I. (1790/2000). *Critique of the Power of Judgment* (A. Wood, Ed.). New York: Cambridge University Press.

Keating, J. (1908). Christianity. In *The Catholic Encyclopedia*. New York: Robert Appleton Company. Retrieved May 1, 2017 from New Advent: http://www.newadvent.org/cathen/03712a.htm

King, P. (2012). Body and Soul. In J. Marenbon (Ed.), *The Oxford Handbook of Medieval Philosophy* (pp. 505–524). New York: Oxford University Press.

Kitcher, P. (1981). Explanatory Unification. *Philosophy of Science, 48*(4), 507–531.

Leiber, J. (1748/1994). Introduction. In J. O. de La Mettrie (Ed.), *Man a Machine and Man a Plant*. Indianapolis, IN: Hackett.

MacIntosh, J., & Anstey, P. (2014, August 18). *Robert Boyle*. Retrieved from Stanford Encyclopedia of Philosophy: http://plato.stanford.edu/entries/boyle/

Marder, M. (2013). *Plant-Thinking: A Philosophy of Vegetal Life*. New York: Columbia University Press.

Mayr, E. (1982). *The Growth of Biological Thought*. Cambridge, MA: Harvard University Press.

McInerny, R., & O'Callaghan, J. (2014, March 23). *Saint Thomas Aquinas*. Retrieved from Stanford Encyclopedia of Philosophy: http://plato.stanford.edu/entries/aquinas/

Mendelson, M. (2010, November 12). *Saint Augustine*. Retrieved from Stanford Encyclopedia of Philosophy: http://plato.stanford.edu/entries/augustine/

Milkowski, M. (2013). *The Computational Theory of Mind*. Retrieved from Internet Encyclopedia of Philosophy: www.iep.utm.edu/compmind/

Multi-Society Task Force on PVS, T. (1994). Medical Aspects of the Persistent Vegetative State. *New England Journal of Medicine, 330*(21), 1499–1508.

Pasnau, R. (2012). Mind and Hylomorphism. In J. Marenbon (Ed.), *The Oxford Handbook of Medieval Philosophy* (pp. 486–504). New York: Oxford University Press.

Piccinini, G. (2009). Computationalism in the Philosophy of Mind. *Philosophy Compass, 9*.

Place, U. (1956). Is Consciousness a Brain Process? *British Journal of Psychology, 47*, 44–50.

Ramsey, W. (2013, April 16). *Eliminative Materialism*. Retrieved from Stanford Encyclopedia of Philosophy: http://plato.stanford.edu/entries/materialism-eliminative/

Rey, G. (1997). *Contemporary Philosophy of Mind*. New York: Blackwell.

Rohlf, M. (2010, May 20). *Immanuel Kant*. Retrieved from Stanford Encyclopedia of Philosophy: http://plato.stanford.edu/entries/kant/

Schneider, S. M., & Morris, E. K. (1987). A History of the Term Radical Behaviorism: From Watson to Skinner. *The Behavior Analyst, 10*(1), 27–39.

Seager, W., & Allen-Hermanson, S. (2010, August 23). *Panpsychism*. Retrieved from Stanford Encyclopedia of Philosophy: http://plato.stanford.edu/entries/panpsychism/

Sellars, W. (1963). Philosophy and the Scientific Image of Man. In W. Sellars (Ed.), *Science, Perception, and Reality* (pp. 1–40). Atascadero, CA: Ridgeview Publishing Co.

Shettleworth, S. (2009). *Cognition, Evolution, and Behavior* (2nd ed.). New York: Oxford University Press.

Shields, C. (2010, August 23). *Aristotle's Psychology*. Retrieved from Stanford Encyclopedia of Philosophy: http://plato.stanford.edu/entries/aristotle-psychology/

Skinner, B. (1945). The Operational Analysis of Psychological Terms. *Psychological Review, 52*, 270–277, 291–294.

Skinner, B. (1953). *Science and Human Behavior*. The Free Press. New York.

Skinner, B. (1963). Behaviorism at Fifty. *Science, 140*, 951–958.

Skrbina, D. (2005). *Panpsychism in the West*. Cambridge, MA: MIT Press.

Smart, J. (1959). Sensations and Brain Processes. *Philosophical Review, 68*, 141–156.

Smart, J. (2007, May 18). *The Mind/Brain Identity Theory*. Retrieved from Stanford Encyclopedia of Philosophy: http://plato.stanford.edu/entries/mind-identity/

Sternberg, R. (2008). *Cognitive Psychology* (5th ed.). Belmont, CA: Wadsworth.

Thomas, K. (1996). *Man and the Natural World*. New York: Oxford University Press.

Thompson, E. (2007). *Mind in Life*. Cambridge, MA: Belknap.

Thorndike, E. (1898). Animal Intelligence. *Psychological Review: Monograph Supplement No.8, 248*, 68–72.

Thorndike, E. (1911). *Animal Intelligence*. New York: Palgrave Macmillan.

Trewavas, A. (2002, February 21). Mindless Mastery. *Nature, 415*, 841.

Trewavas, A. (2004). Aspects of Plant Intelligence: An Answer to Firn. *Annals of Botany, 93*(4), 353–357.

van Gelder, T. (1995). What Might Cognition Be, If Not Computation? *The Journal of Philosophy, 92*(7), 345–381.

Watson, J. B. (1913). Psychology as the Behaviorist Views It. *Psychological Review, 20*, 158–177.

Weber, A., & Varela, F. (2002). Life After Kant. *Phenomenology and the Cognitive Sciences, 1*, 97–125.

Weiner, J. (1994). *The Beak of the Finch*. New York: Vintage.

Whippo, C. W., & Hangarter, R. P. (2009). The 'Sensational' Power of Movement in Plants. *American Journal of Botany, 96*(12), 2115–2127.

2 Perceiving

1. Naïve Admiration

I grew up admiring flowers, daffodils especially (Figure 2.1). My father loved growing and showing them in competitions. I have an amalgamated memory of crouching near our few flower beds in a suburb of Washington, D.C., peering closely at their petals, cups, and stems, listening as he explained what made this one special, unusual. He baffled me with his ability to notice things that I only barely noticed even with his help—such as an irregular edge of a petal. A few times he took me and my sister to a daffodil competition, where there were rows and rows of different but all seemingly perfect specimens. Orange cups, salmon cups, pink cups, long cups, short cups, crisp white petals, gold petals, buttery petals, rounded petals, and pointy petals. How could the judges—one of which my dad eventually became—reasonably choose which were truly the best? My dad also took us to the home of the daffodil lady, as I thought of her. She tended several enormous beds of daffodils, numbering in the thousands. While she talked with my father, I and my sister would wander around, sometimes noticing particular flowers, more often hoping to go inside for some lemonade. At some point, my dad told us that the lady (Marie Bozievich) was nationally renowned for her care of daffodils.[1] I liked best the ones with the blown-back petals, which looked like they were cruising in a convertible.

A lot of what my dad said about daffodils was lost on me, but I did think they were beautiful. They could just as well have been crafted by artisans, rather than independently growing organisms. I knew basic things about plants: that we grow them for food, spices, medicine, clothing, and building materials; that they rely on something called 'photosynthesis'; that they consume carbon dioxide and release oxygen. But I didn't really consider what it took for them to live.

It was many years later, while researching some finer points about philosophical theories of the mind, that I got wondering about plants. It dawned

Figure 2.1 Daffodil (*Narcissus poeticus*)

on me that some of the most prominent, contemporary theorists of mind believe that plants think.[2] That's when I started to look further into biology. While exploring textbooks, I came across Daniel Chamowitz's *What a Plant Knows*. Chamowitz, a plant biologist, reports what plant biologists apparently have known for a long time: although plants generally stay in one place (they're 'sessile'), they are very sensitive, even active, constantly negotiating their environments.[3] It's not just that their cells, like all living cells, are constantly doing things. It's rather that whole plants or their parts—their roots, shoots, and leaves—do things in response to their environment.

We all know that plants use sunlight. With its help, they convert water and carbon dioxide into energy. But plants don't just get or fail to get sunlight. Most seek it. They grow towards it. If a light source illuminates one side of, say, an oat seedling for long enough, that seedling will in time noticeably bend toward the source. If the light source moves to the other side of the seedling, the seedling will in time bend in that direction. This is phototropism. In general, a tropism is an oriented response to a stimulus. In phototropism, the plant does not merely respond to the stimulus of light—say, by starting photosynthesis—instead, it responds to the direction of the stimulus, either towards it (positive phototropism) or away from it (negative phototropism). The phenomenon is very common.[4]

Consider another tropism. You don't need to be a plant biologist to see that the stem of a flower grows up out of the soil, while the roots grow down into it. In this, they are like most plants. Shoots go up; roots go down. Perfectly familiar, but actually a bit curious. It can seem that shoots grow up simply because they are rigid. They're stiff and generally straight, so they just stand up, rather than, say, lie on their side. But that doesn't explain anything: their rigidity could just as well force shoots downward, into the soil. Indeed, roots grow down into the soil. Of course, if the whole plant grew down into the soil, it wouldn't get enough or any sunlight. But how does the plant know that? Same goes for roots. Why don't they grow up out of the soil? (Sometimes they do, but not in general.) They need to be in the soil to tap water and nutrients, and to anchor the plant, but how do they figure that out? These behaviors are instances of gravitropism, an oriented response to the direction of gravity. Roots exhibit positive gravitropism, growing with or towards the direction of gravity. Shoots exhibit negative gravitropism, growing against the direction of gravity.

Darwin said, "No one can look at plants growing on a bank or on the borders of a thick wood, and doubt that the young stems and leaves place themselves so that the leaves may be well illuminated."[5] Obvious though it might have been to Darwin, in real time, phototropism and gravitropism are hard for us to see; they're slow. Time-lapse video makes it much easier to see. Surely the fact that plants *move* in these ways is surprising. I mean, if someone told you plants move, you'd probably think she was loony, or that she simply meant that plants are flexible, able to bend under pressure. And "move" and "movement" are indeed how plant biologists often talk about tropisms.[6]

It now seems obvious to me that plants must move. They are alive, after all. That is strangely easy to forget. Most plants, including daffodils in my family's old yard, start as mere seeds, but become relatively enormous and elaborate structures. That takes energy and nutrients. If those things are not immediately available, plants must find them, or die. Growing haphazardly or aimlessly won't do. Indeed, phototropism and gravitropism make it seem as if daffodils (and other plants) somehow perceive their environment, seeking what's good for them, what they need. Do they perceive?

2. What Are Plants?

To appreciate the ways that plants respond to their environment, it helps to know some basic facts about their anatomy and evolution.

Centuries ago, in his *Systema Naturae* of 1735, Carolus Linnaeus (1707–1778) classified organisms simply into animals and plants, but biologists have learned a lot since then. Although they continue to debate how properly to classify organisms, many biologists now recognize two domains, Prokaryota and Eukaryota, which are divided further into six kingdoms: Bacteria, Archaea, Protista, Plantae, Fungi, and Animalia.

Along with protists, fungi, and animals, plants are eukaryotes, which evolved from prokaryotes, which emerged roughly 3.6 billion years ago. Bacteria and archaea are prokaryotes; they are generally single-celled

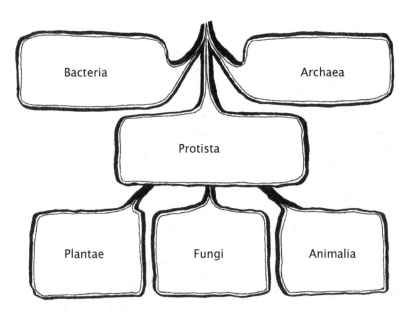

Figure 2.2 Six kingdoms of organisms

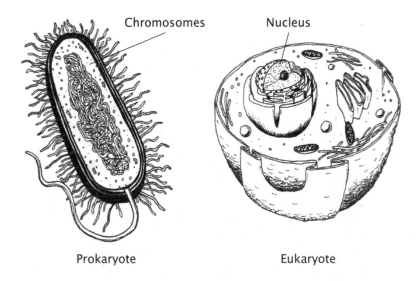

Chromosomes Nucleus

Prokaryote Eukaryote

Figure 2.3 Schematic prokaryote and eukaryote cells

organisms. Their cells have no nucleus, no membrane-bound organelle which houses their chromosomes, the super-coiled filaments of DNA (Figure 2.3). Counting sheer numbers of individual organisms, bacteria are by far the most populous organism on earth. In a single human's intestine, for instance, there are billions of individual bacteria, aiding in digestion and immunity to disease.[7] By contrast, currently there are about seven billion humans on earth. Plants, however, are estimated to constitute the majority of the total biomass of the earth.[8]

Eukaryotes have a nucleus, an organelle housing their chromosomes. A leading hypothesis—the endosymbiotic theory made prominent by Lynn Margulis—holds that roughly two billion years ago, eukaryotes resulted from prokaryotes consuming one another.[9] This was a mutually beneficial, symbiotic relationship. Via this process, there came to be cells with mitochondria, an organelle dedicated to producing energy for the rest of the cell. Also via this process, some eukaryotes eventually came to have chloroplasts, organelles dedicated to converting carbon dioxide and water, in the presence of light, into fuel (sugar, glucose specifically), to be consumed subsequently by mitochondria. Plants are made of these sorts of cells.

I have been talking simply of plants, as if they are all the same, when in fact they are impressively diverse. There are mosses, ferns, sequoias, and daffodils. Likewise, talking simply of animals also risks confusion,

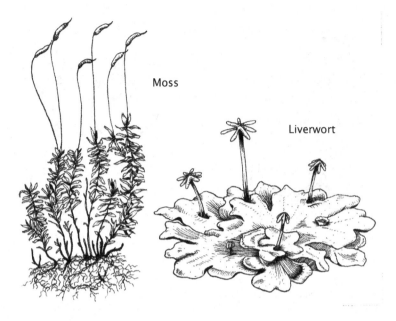

Figure 2.4 Moss and liverwort

since very different things count as animals: earthworms, clams, fruit flies, finches, and humans.

Contemporary botanists distinguish between vascular and non-vascular plants. Vascular plants have xylem, tissue dedicated to transporting water within the plant. Non-vascular plants don't have xylem. Non-vascular plants, such as mosses and liverworts, evolved first, before vascular plants, such as sequoias and daffodils (Figure 2.4).

The vast majority of plants are vascular. Their tissues are typically arranged concentrically, one sort of tissue nested within another, roughly like a series of cylinders (Figure 2.5). Cells of different tissues are different; some have stronger walls, providing support; others have special coatings, providing protection, or impeding movement of certain substances; others are for transporting substances, such as water. Most vascular plants have roots, shoots, and leaves. Roots anchor the plant, also supplying it with water and minerals absorbed from the soil. These are then transported to the rest of the plant through the xylem, tissues of dead cells that are roughly tube-like, connected end to end, extending upward through the shoot and outward to the branches. The xylems are commonly arrayed in a ring around the center (the pith) of the plant. Leaves are the primary site

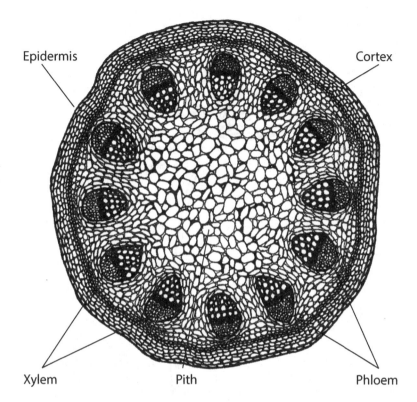

Epidermis

Cortex

Xylem

Pith

Phloem

Figure 2.5 Cross-section of stereotypical stem

of photosynthesis, which generates food (glucose) for the plant. This food moves to the rest of the plant through the phloem, which is similar to the xylem, forming a ring of channels ordinarily positioned just outside the xylem. Together, the xylem and phloem count as the vascular system. Plants with such a system are vascular plants.

The majority of vascular plants bear seeds and flower. A seed is a fertilized egg of a plant in a protective coating. Seeds allow plants to propagate across great distances, borne by wind or water or sometimes stuck to other organisms, like deer. Flowers are the reproductive parts of the plant, the sex organs. Normally, flowers have both 'male' and 'female' parts, ones that can produce a small gamete (pollen) and a large gamete (egg) (Figure 2.6). Flowers make it easier for one plant to fertilize or be fertilized by a different plant of the same species (cross-fertilization), which has the effect

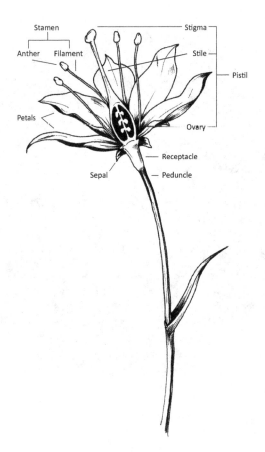

Figure 2.6 Parts of a stereotypical flower

of creating variety in the next generation of that plant. Because flowering plants are the most common, in the rest of the book, I will focus on them.

Knowing a little about evolution—for instance, that sophisticated organisms evolved later than simple organisms—it is tempting to think that plants came before animals, but the truth is more interesting than that (Figure 2.7). Green algae, precursors to plants, emerged well before early animals, earthworm-like creatures. But early land plants (mosses) came forty million years after early, jawless fish. And flowering plants emerged well after early mammals—mice-like creatures—and early birds.[10] So, if later organisms are more sophisticated than earlier organisms, then land plants are more sophisticated than early fish, and flowering plants are more sophisticated than early fish, early mammals, and early birds!

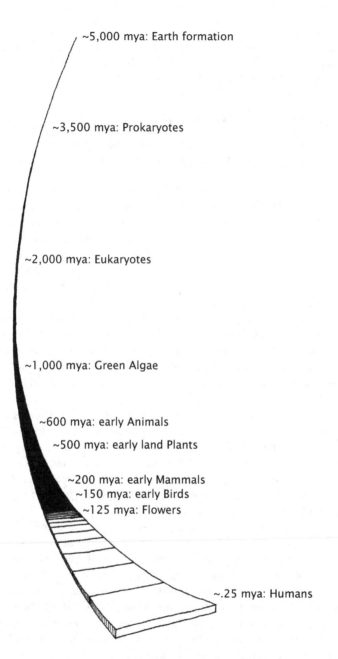

Figure 2.7 Timeline of the emergence of life on Earth (mya = million years ago)

We should, however, be careful: it is not really clear what 'sophisticated' means in this context, so we should not hastily agree that later organisms are necessarily more sophisticated than earlier ones. Still, it is a mistake to think simply that plants came before animals.

3. Phototropism and Gravitropism

With those basics in place, now consider how phototropism (oriented growth in response to light) and gravitropism (oriented growth in response to gravity) work.

Already in the fourth century B.C.E, Theophrastus, one of Aristotle's students, noticed phototropism.[11] He speculated that it was a sort of wilting induced by the sun. Only in the seventeenth century, 2,000 years later, did some people start experimenting to figure out what exactly was happening. Possibly the first to do so was Thomas Browne (1605–1682), who thought it might be a response to the "bad air" emitted by neighboring plants.[12] He found that when mustard seedlings grown near a window had their pot turned away from the window, they would orient towards it. In his mind, the seedlings were drawn to it by the good air. John Ray (1627–1705), arguably the most influential botanist of the second half of the 1600s, disagreed, contending that phototropism wasn't due to bad air, but to different temperatures on different sides of the plant: the side closest to the window was cooler and therefore grew more slowly than the other side, causing the plant to bend.[13]

But these movements are tied not to heat but light, as Charles Darwin and his son Francis discovered. They published their results in 1880 in *The Power of Movement in Plants*. Using canary grass seedlings, they showed first that when the tip or apex of the shoot is removed, there is no bending towards light, suggesting that the tip is necessary for bending. To be sure that the lack of response was not merely a result of damage to the plant, they next left the tip intact, but covered it with an opaque cap. Again, when exposed to light, the seedlings didn't bend. To rule out the possibility that mere physical contact with the apex wasn't the cause of the lack of bending, they did a third experiment, using transparent caps. This time, they observed bending. But it was possible that putting an opaque cover on just any part of the plant would impede bending. So, in a fourth experiment, they covered the stems of the seedlings, not the tip, and found that the seedlings still bent towards the light. Together, these experiments suggested that the apex of the shoot is where the light source is detected, initiating the bending response further down the shoot[14] (Figure 2.8).

In 1910, Peter Boysen-Jensen showed that something soluble was transmitted from the apex to the stem.[15] When one substance (mica) was placed

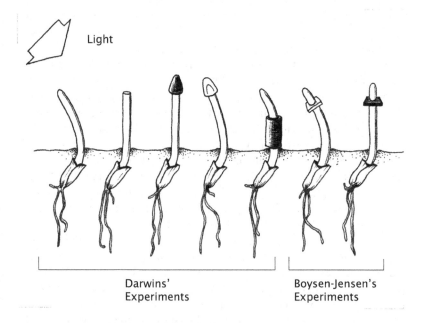

Light

Darwins'
Experiments

Boysen-Jensen's
Experiments

Figure 2.8 The Darwins' and Boysen-Jensen's experiments

between the tip and the rest of the shoot, there was no bending. But when another substance (gelatin) was used instead, there was bending. Whatever the "messenger" was, it could pass through the second but not the first. Boysen-Jensen also showed that when mica was placed on only the dark side of the plant, there was no bending, which suggested that bending required transmission of a substance from the apex to the dark side of the shoot. In 1926, Fritz Went isolated this substance, dubbing it "auxin," deriving from the ancient Greek word 'auxanein,' which means to increase. Cells exposed to more auxin expand (up to a limit). Went and Nicolai Cholodny proposed that at the tip, auxin is transported laterally from the illuminated side to the dark side. Although the precise nature of this transmission is still being studied, the Went-Cholodny theory is widely accepted.[16] As auxin increases in the cells on the dark side of the plant, that side grows more than the light side, causing the characteristic curvature of phototropism.

The history of gravitropism is murkier than that of phototropism. In 1806, Thomas Knight reported that he had followed up observations made in 1758 by Henri-Louis Duhamel de Monceau. Although Knight said that the shoots-up–roots-down phenomenon could not escape even "the most inattentive observer," it is not clear when it was first seen as worthy of explanation.[17] (Before the recognition of gravity, for instance, how might one have tried to explain it?) Knight performed a nifty experiment to test his hypothesis that gravity was the main cause. He fastened several soaked seeds around an upright wheel, which he then rotated with a stream of water at a rate of 150 rotations per minute (Figures 2.9 and 2.10). (Eventually this sort of device was replaced with a clinostat.) As he predicted, a few days later the seeds began to germinate, with the shoots growing toward the center of the wheel, while the roots grew outward. Shoots grew against the direction of the centrifugal force, while roots grew with it. Knight performed a similar experiment with a horizontal wheel. Also as he predicted, the shoots did not grow straight up, and the roots did not grow straight down, but angled away from the center of the wheel. From this, Knight concluded that gravity was indeed the main cause of shoots-up–roots-down.

But, as Knight himself appreciated, how could one and the same force "produce effects so diametrically opposite to each other"?[18]

The Darwins investigated gravitropism in roots, and found that the root cap is essential for it to occur. They hypothesized that the root cap is where the plant senses gravity. When they removed it, roots didn't bend downward. Although that helped clarify what was happening with the roots, it didn't explain why there was "diametrically opposite" growth in shoots.[19]

In 1900, it was hypothesized that the bits sensitive to gravity, generically called "statoliths," are amyoplasts, subcellular bodies that "sediment" or

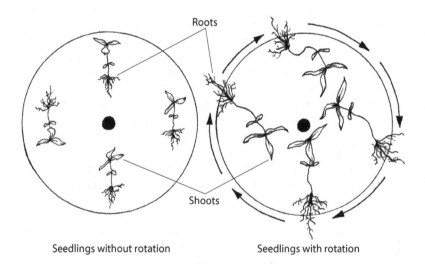

Seedlings without rotation   Seedlings with rotation

Figure 2.9 Thomas Knight's device for studying gravitropism

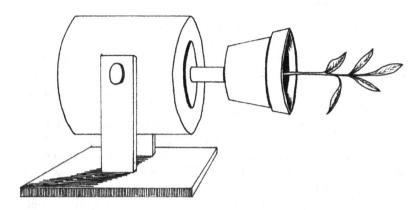

Figure 2.10 Clinostat

accumulate at the bottom of special cells, "statocytes," in the tips of both roots and shoots.[20] Although there have been challenges to it, a version of that hypothesis is widely taken as correct.[21] The amyoplasts are somewhat denser than the rest of the cell, and will accordingly "sediment" on the bottom of the cell. They're like rocks in a jug of water; turn the jug, and the rocks will drift to the bottom. (A similar mechanism exists in our inner ear, part of our vestibular system, helping us recognize whether we are upright or not.) When the amyoplasts settle on the bottom of the cell, as proposed by Went and Cholodny, auxin is transmitted to another part of the plant, causing differential growth.

But what about that "diametrically opposite" growth? It turns out that "auxin" is a misnomer since it does not simply stimulate growth of cells; it does so only up to certain thresholds, beyond which it *inhibits* growth. In a horizontally oriented shoot, the settled amyoplasts cause transmission of auxin to the underside of the shoot, where cells expand at a faster rate than those on the top side, causing the whole shoot to bend upward. Something different happens with roots. In a horizontally oriented root, auxin is also transmitted to the underside, but it does not stimulate expansion there; rather, it inhibits it. Consequently, cells on the top side of the root expand faster, causing the root to bend downward. The "diametrically opposite" growth of shoots and roots is due to the effects of different concentrations of auxin in shoots and roots.[22]

To figure out whether phototropism and gravitropism involve perception, we need now to look more closely at perception.

4. What Is Perception?

Put this book down; take stock of what you perceive.

To my right I see a cup, sitting on a brown desk. It's green, shiny, cylindrical. Voices I hear from behind me, from another room. Inhaling deeply, I smell coffee, toothpaste, shampoo, and humidity. Toothpaste lingers in my mouth. Placing my hand on my leg, I feel warmth, and the modestly coarse texture of my jeans. My chair pushes against my back and butt.

We perceive lots of things, of different sorts, through our five senses, or "modalities," as they're called by people who study these things: vision, hearing, smell, taste, and touch. We also have a sixth sense, proprioception, our sense of our body's orientation (upright, rather than prone), and of the position of our parts relative to one another.

Perception involves being affected, but to perceive a thing isn't simply to be affected by it. In seeing the cup, the cup affects me. More exactly, light reflected from the cup affects me. But seeing the cup requires more than simply being affected by it. Think of the vast array of things currently affecting you. Think of the bacteria all over your skin. They certainly affect you—they exert a modest pressure on you—but you do not perceive them. And even now as you contemplate that fact, you do not perceive them; you cannot see or feel them. (Granted, at an intellectual level, you perceive these facts. You *comprehend* that you are being so affected, but that is something else.) There are lots of cases like that, of one thing being affected by another, without perceiving it. As the temperature rises on a winter day, and the sun shines, ice on the ground melts. But patches of ice don't perceive rising temperatures or the sun. Perception involves something more than simply being affected. When we perceive something, we notice it, or recognize it, or are aware of it in some way. When I perceive the cup on my desk, I am aware of it. I might not be aware of everything about it—I don't see its weight, its origin, or its molecular structure—but I am aware of some things about it, like its being a cup.

What is the difference between perceiving X and simply being affected by X?

Aristotle thought that perception was like a seal being pressed into wax.[23] The thing perceived (the cup) impresses itself on the perceiver (me), imparting something of itself to the perceiver, its form. David Hume (1711–1776), the very influential Scottish philosopher, also embraced this analogy.[24] His name for perceptions was "impressions." That captures the idea that in perception, we 'take in' some aspect of the thing perceived.

When we perceive something, it appears to us as being some way or other, as having this or that feature. When I see my green coffee cup, it appears to me *as a cup*; that's how it looks to me. Perception involves portrayal, portraying something *as* being *of some sort*. For this reason, perception seems to involve classifying, or categorizing. This classifying is not deliberate: I don't think about or plan to do it. Nor is it conscious: I am not aware that it is happening. It just happens, automatically. Shut your eyes for a few seconds, and then open them. Things just strike you in various ways: as being this big, that far away, this color, that shape.

One difficult question is how much of this classifying happens in perception itself, and how much of it happens after perception, in thought.[25] Several paragraphs back, I took stock of some things I perceive, reporting it to you in words. But perception ordinarily involves just perceiving things, not paying attention to what you're perceiving and then describing it for others. This process of paying attention to what I perceive, and then describing it, potentially distorts what I perceive—by adding to or subtracting from what I really perceive.[26] For instance, when I visually perceive the cup, maybe all I genuinely perceive is its color (green) and shape (cylinder); perhaps recognition that it is a cup happens only later, after perception, in thought. Despite that complication, many still believe that at least some classifying or categorizing—some recognition of features—does occur in perception itself.

Now, my cup might feel empty when it isn't. Things are not always as they seem to us to be. So, although all perceptions portray a thing as being this way or that way, not all perceptions portray things accurately.

Because perception involves portrayal, sometimes inaccurate portrayal, most scientists and philosophers think that it involves representation.[27] That it does so gives us a way to distinguish between perceiving a thing and simply being affected by it; one involves representation, the other doesn't. Traditionally, the basic idea was that in the case of visual perception, we form an image, a picture, of the thing perceived. As even kids know, when you look into a person's eye, very closely, there you will see an image of yourself. Indeed, in general, when we see something, an image of it forms on our eye. Earlier thinkers speculated that some version of this image is transmitted further inside of us and, somehow, culminates in perception of the thing. Sometimes this image, this representation, is accurate; sometimes it is inaccurate or misleading, thus accounting for the possibility of misperception.

In your average college psychology textbook or perception textbook, you will find an updated version of this story that goes as follows.[28] We must distinguish between stimulus, sensation, and perception[29] (Figure 2.11). The stimulus is a source of energy, such as my green, shiny coffee cup. Sensation is the initial effect, such as the stimulation of my retina, the part of my eye behind the iris and lens. It is also common to refer to the source of energy as the 'distal stimulus,' and to sensation as the 'proximal stimulus.' Perception is the interpretation of the sensation, classifying it in some way,

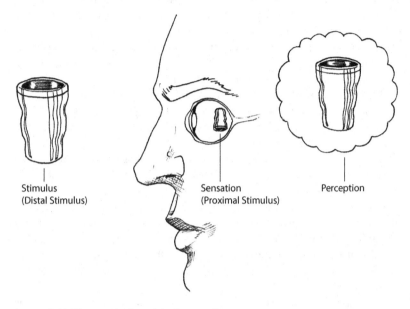

Figure 2.11 The standard model of perception

and in turn portraying the (distal) stimulus as being this or that way—for instance, green, cylindrical, near. That is only the roughest summary of a much more elaborate story. What matters most is that scientists and philosophers think that perception necessarily involves *representation*.

Given that this is the dominant way of thinking about perception, let us see where it leads when thinking about plants.[30]

5. Do Plants Perceive?

Do phototropism or gravitropism involve perception? More precisely, do they involve forming *representations* (of, say, light or gravity)?

It's plausible. The sun itself does not arrive at the plant, but exerts itself on the plant by electromagnetic radiation, which makes an initial impact on some part of the plant, the 'photoreceptors,' specialized parts of cells that are distinctively sensitive to light. These initial effects are arguably representations of the sun: not just a signal from the sun, but a sign of the sun. They are, one might say, more or less, like the images formed on the lens of our eyes when we see something. Although we see no image on the surface of a plant when it is being affected by the sun, there is nevertheless something comparable going on—even if it is harder to detect, or not easily seen.

That way of thinking relies on a particular conception of what a representation is, of what it is for one thing—such as an image or word—to represent another. Roughly, the idea is that if X causes Y, then Y represents X. For example, wet pavement caused by rain represents or is a sign of rain; a hoofprint of a deer is a representation or sign of a deer; smoke is a representation or sign of fire. This is the Causal Theory of Representation[31] (Figure 2.12).

That might seem to be a sensible way to think about representation, but for a couple reasons, it is widely regarded as problematic.

First, the Causal Theory of Representation implies that every effect is a representation. Pick anything that has a cause. Look around you: that chair, that granola bar, that piece of sidewalk, that hair on your right hand, that speck of dirt, that wispy tail on that cloud. The Causal Theory says that each is also a representation, a representation of its cause. But that doesn't seem true. Aren't only some things—such as pictures and statements—representations? Accepting the Causal Theory would force us to accept not only that more things are representations than we might initially have thought, but also that everything that has a cause is a representation.

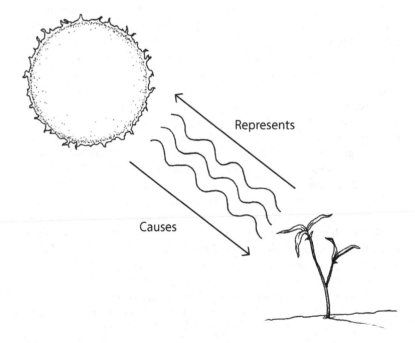

Figure 2.12 The Causal Theory of Representation. The sun has an effect on the plant, an effect which represents the sun.

Effects are not necessarily representations—of their causes, or of anything else. The paradigm of a representation is a picture or a statement, each capable of portraying something as being some way or other. A photograph of wet pavement portrays some pavement as wet. The statement "The pavement is wet" likewise portrays some pavement as wet. An effect of some event, however, is not necessarily a portrayal of anything at all. Suppose that some wet pavement is indeed an effect of recent rain. The wet pavement is not, therefore, a picture of or statement about rain. It does not depict or say anything about rain. It does not portray rain. True, a person who knew about rain and its effects could use the wet pavement as evidence that it might have recently rained, but that does not imply that wet pavement represents—depicts, says something about, portrays—rain. Exactly the same thing can be said of hoofprints and smoke. In general, Y can be an effect of X without being a representation of X.

A second problem with the Causal Theory of Representation is that it guarantees, by definition, that every representation is accurate. The Theory thus makes misrepresentation impossible; there is no possibility for a representation to inaccurately represent what it represents. If X causes Y, then Y represents X, but so long as Y always has a cause, it will always be accurate. If Y has no cause, it represents nothing at all. The very thing that causes Y to occur is also what it represents, thus ensuring that it is always accurate. For instance, suppose your doorbell rings as the result of a short circuit. We should like to say that it misrepresents the presence of someone at your door; it signals that someone is there, when no one is. Yet the Causal Theory of Representation must say that the ringing bell does not misrepresent. It represents exactly what it was caused by, namely, the short circuit. Thus, the Causal Theory makes misrepresentation impossible. But misrepresentation clearly is possible. Not every representation is accurate. Some portraits of Darwin are not faithful to the man. Some statements about Darwin's exploits aboard the HMS *Beagle* are false, such as the claim that he there first conjured his theory of natural selection while contemplating his finches. Furthermore, even if it happened—by great care or just dumb luck—that every single representation turned out to be accurate, that bizarre eventuality should not be guaranteed simply by one's theory or definition of what a representation is. A good theory of representation—of what representations are—should preserve the possibility that some representations misrepresent.

So, in trying to figure out whether plants perceive, and whether phototropism or gravitropism involve representation, we should not rely on the Causal Theory.

At this point, it is natural to look for another, better theory of representation. There are other theories, and some are modestly better, but they are also generally regarded as very problematic. Despite a lot of ingenuity and effort, there is no consensus on what it takes for something to be a representation. That's surprising, given how utterly common and important representations are; we're surrounded by images and words. Most theorists think the trouble in getting a good theory stems from misrepresentation, from trying to tell the right story about that unique sort of error. We don't need to go into those details right now, but in later chapters, we will return to representations, for they are the heart of the case against plant minds.

Consider instead when it makes sense to *hypothesize* that representation is involved in some behavior, when it makes sense to propose that a creature is relying on a representation to do something. Since the nineteenth century, psychologists have been studying perception in nonhuman animals. They have devised a suite of experiments for doing so. A common strategy is to test for changes of behavior with changes in stimuli. For instance, hamsters mark territories with scents, which other hamsters then vigorously sniff. They sniff less vigorously when they consistently encounter the scent from the same individual. They 'habituate' to that scent. But they resume sniffing vigorously when they encounter a scent from a different individual. They 'dishabituate' from the first scent. That change in vigor is taken to show that the hamsters discriminate between scents of different individuals.[32] This sort of discriminatory behavior by itself does not show that animals form representations of things that affect them. (Responding differently to different stimuli need not involve a representation. A puddle gets warmer when the air warms, but does not rely on a representation of air temperature in doing so.) But this sort of test is the basis for more sophisticated tests, which give good reasons for thinking that many animals do indeed form representations of things that affect them, and, thus, that they do not merely sense those things, but genuinely perceive them.[33]

Think about a hungry dog and a bone. Turn the bone this way and that. Place it far away from the dog. Place it close. Place it to the left of the dog, then to the right. Place it in less light, or in more. In each case, the dog's response will be essentially similar: it will salivate. There is something intriguing here. Through all of these changes in position, the proximal stimuli—the immediate effect of the bone on the eyes of the dog—also change widely, while the bone, the distal stimulus, remains the same. In particular, the angle and intensity of light arriving at the dog's eyes varies substantially. The image on the lens of the dog's eyes varies considerably. Despite those differences in the proximal stimuli, the dog's responses are the same. How can that be? Well, the sameness of response cannot be explained by the sameness of the proximal stimuli, for they are not the same. Somehow, widely different proximal stimuli elicit the same type of response from the dog.

Vision scientists hypothesize that a representation mediates between the proximal stimuli and the response. Different proximal stimuli can result in the same response because they generate a single type of representation, a representation of the distal stimulus—of the bone, in our example—which in turn controls the response. Across the changes in the bone's position, location, and angle relative to the dog, the dog continues to perceive the bone as the same.

This ability to regard an object as unchanging across changes in that object's location, orientation, and illumination is known as perceptual constancy.[34] It is a mundane aspect of our daily lives. It is at work when we approach, say, a daffodil and it continues to look the same size, despite a relative increase in the size of the images on the lenses of our eyes. The daffodil takes up a bigger and bigger portion of our visual field, but we don't thereby see it as a bigger daffodil, one that grows as we get closer. (This is known more specifically as size constancy.) Somehow, we—our brains, our bodies—just figure this out, automatically and unconsciously. And it's not just us and dogs that are capable of perceptual constancy, but a huge number of animals, including fish and bees. It is necessary for these creatures to move about in the world without every movement implying that the world itself has changed.

Thus, one way to check whether plants form representations—and so perceive, rather than merely sense things—would be to check for constancy. Do plants exhibit it?

We need something similar to our dog-and-bone example, a plant exhibiting a constancy of response to a single object despite changes to that object's location or orientation. Consider *phototorsion*, twisting toward light, as seen in sunflowers. As the sun changes position, the flower has a constant reaction: orienting towards the sun. While the sun changes position, the flower exhibits a constancy of response; it consistently turns toward. So, phototorsion might seem to involve constancy.

But this appearance is misleading, trading on loose use of words. It is misleading to say that because the flower always twists as the sun changes position, the flower displays 'the same' response. Although it is indeed true that the flower twists when the sun moves, the important thing is that changes in the sun's position elicit different responses from the flower. When the sun is *here*, the flower orients *this way*; when it's *there*, it orients *that way*. The flower's twisting can be explained almost wholly in terms of the proximal stimuli, the angle and intensity of electromagnetic radiation hitting some part of the flower. It is not necessary to hypothesize that a representation mediates between the proximal stimuli and the twisting response, for different proximal stimuli do *not* result in the same response. Phototorsion is not evidence of perceptual constancy.

By itself, this point does *not* show that plants definitely do *not* form representations of things they respond to. It shows only that we do not yet have reason to think their behaviors involve perceptual constancy. Are there other reasons for hypothesizing that plants form representations of what they respond to?

It can seem so. Typically, when a light is moved or removed entirely, a plant will continue to grow in the direction of the previous location of the light. John Ray showed this in his early experiments on phototropism.[35] In this respect, the plant can appear to be making a mistake, growing in the wrong direction, growing in a direction where there is no light.[36] That can tempt us to think that it is misperceiving the environment—hence, that it is misrepresenting where there is light, representing it as being-over-there, when it isn't.

Botanists rightly tend not to think of it that way. They don't think of this sort of behavior as growth in response to an absence of light. Instead, they think of it as the delayed cessation of a response (growth) to the presence of light. The plant is not here responding to the absence of light by growing. Indeed, after enough exposure to the absence of light from a certain direction, the plant will cease growing in that direction. If the light is positioned elsewhere, the plant will start growing in that direction. Thus, it would be a mistake to think that to do this, the plant must have a representation of light as being-over-there.

6. Unperceptive Plants

Where does all of this put us? Phototropism and gravitropism suggest that plants might perceive their environment. The currently dominant way of thinking about perception requires representation. Perception of X, rather than mere stimulation by X, requires forming a representation of X. So, if plants perceive things, they must represent those things. However, looking more closely at phototropism, we have not yet found good reason to believe that it involves representation. I think the same can be said for gravitropism. Thus, if we accept the dominant way of thinking, plants don't perceive.

But, you might say, plants *should* count as capable of perceiving, so we should reject the dominant way of thinking about perception. It is unsatisfying to say that plants don't perceive, for that seems to imply they are like rocks and puddles, merely responsive to stimuli. And surely they are different! It's not enough to say that plants are alive but rocks and puddles aren't. That's obvious. We want to be able to say how *the responses themselves* are different. Perhaps the three-part distinction between stimulus, sensation, and perception is inadequate. Maybe there's some other category, or distinction.

Another possibility is that when plants sense things, it feels some way to them. For instance, green looks a certain way to us, and coffee has a certain smell. Do plants feel things, in that sense?

Notes

1 Marie—as my dad fondly refers to her—was also outstanding in other ways, designing and creating two of the American Daffodil Society's sterling silver trophies (ADS, 1980).
2 Preparing for a presentation at Washington and Lee University in November 2013, titled "Varieties of Minds," I was thinking specifically about (Millikan, 1984) and (Dretske, 1989).
3 "Restless plants" is the theme of (Keller, 2011).
4 See, for instance, (Bidlack & Jansky, 2010) and (Scott, 2008).
5 (Darwin & Darwin, 1880, p. 449); quoted in (Christie & Murphy, 2013, p. 35).
6 See, for instance, (Bidlack & Jansky, 2010) and (Scott, 2008).
7 (Whitman, Coleman, & Wiebe, 1998). For a downward revision of previous estimates of the biomass of marine bacteria, see (Kallmeyer, Pockalny, Adhikari, Smith, & D'Hondt, 2012).
8 For instance, (Scott, 2008, p. 17).
9 (Margulis, 1967) and (Margulis, 1981).
10 (Lucas & Luo, 1993).
11 (Morton, 1981).
12 (Whippo & Hangarter, 2006, p. 111).
13 (Morton, 1981, p. 195).
14 (Whippo & Hangarter, 2006).
15 (Scott, 2008).
16 See, for instance, (Scott, 2008) and (Christie & Murphy, 2013).
17 (Knight, 1806, p. 99).
18 (Knight, 1806, p. 99).
19 See, for instance, (Chen, Rosen, & Masson, 1999), (Scott, 2008), (Whippo & Hangarter, 2009), and (Bidlack & Jansky, 2010).
20 (Chen, Rosen, & Masson, 1999).
21 (Blancaflor & Masson, 2003) and (Bidlack & Jansky, 2010).
22 See, for instance, (Chen, Rosen, & Masson, 1999), (Blancaflor & Masson, 2003), (Scott, 2008), and (Bidlack & Jansky, 2010).
23 (Aristotle, 1984/1995).
24 (Hume, 1739/1985).
25 See, for instance, (Carey, 2009) and (Siegel, 2010).
26 See, for instance, (Sokolowski, 1999) and (Thompson & Zahavi, 2007).
27 See, for instance, (Palmer, 1999), (Sternberg, 2008), (Goldstein, 2009), (Shettleworth, 2009) (Zimbardo, Johnson, & Hamilton, 2011), and (Crane, 2011).
28 See, for instance, (Palmer, 1999), (Sternberg, 2008), (Goldstein, 2009), (Shettleworth, 2009), and (Zimbardo, Johnson, & Hamilton, 2011).
29 For a good, brief history of the stimulus-sensation-perception distinction, see (Ben-Zeev, 1984).
30 Some philosophers worry that this is not the right way to think about perception. See, for instance, (Noe, 2004).
31 See, for instance, (Adams & Aizawa, 2010).

32 (Shettleworth, 2009, p. 62).
33 As I will discuss in Chapter Five, there are other things that animals do that seem to require representations. For instance, in Ivan Pavlov's famous experiments, after a dog has learned that a bell is associated with food, the dog salivates upon hearing that bell (Pavlov, 1928). Some psychologists have thought that the bell produces a representation of food, which in turn causes the salivation. Another famous example is Edward Tolman's rats, who, after having successfully navigated a maze, were able to find novel shortcuts through it (Tolman, 1948). Tolman proposed that they rely on cognitive maps in doing so. See also (Shettleworth, 2009).
34 (Palmer, 1999), (Sternberg, 2008), (Goldstein, 2009), and (Zimbardo, Johnson, & Hamilton, 2011). For a more philosophical discussion, see (Cohen, Forthcoming).
35 (Morton, 1981).
36 Some plants regularly exhibit negative phototropism, growth away from a light source. For these plants, such growth is typically beneficial, helping them avoid damage or over-heating.

Works Cited

Adams, F., & Aizawa, K. (2010, February 4). *Causal Theories of Mental Content.* Retrieved from Stanford Encyclopedia of Philosophy: http://plato.stanford.edu/entries/content-causal/
ADS. (1980). Citation for the Award of the Silver Medal of the ADS. *The Daffodil Journal, 16*(4), 203.
Aristotle. (1984/1995). On the Soul. In Aristotle & J. Barnes (Ed.), *The Complete Works of Aristotle*. Princeton, NJ: Princeton University Press.
Ben-Zeev, A. (1984). The Passivity Assumption of the Sensation-Perception Distinction. *The British Journal for the Philosophy of Science, 35*(4), 327–343.
Bidlack, J., & Jansky, S. (2010). *Stern's Introductory Plant Biology* (12th ed.). New York: McGraw-Hill.
Blancaflor, E., & Masson, P. (2003). Plant Gravitropism: Unraveling the Ups and Downs of a Complex Process. *Plant Physiology, 133*, 1677–1690.
Carey, S. (2009). *The Origin of Concepts*. New York: Oxford University Press.
Chen, R., Rosen, E., & Masson, P. (1999). Gravitropism in Higher Plants. *Plant Physiology*, 343–350.
Christie, J. M., & Murphy, A. S. (2013). Shoot Phototropism in Higher Plants. *American Journal of Botany, 100*(1), 35–46.
Cohen, J. (Forthcoming). Perceptual Constancy. In M. Matthen (Ed.), *Oxford Handbook of the Philosophy of Perception*. New York: Oxford University Press.
Crane, T. (2011, February 4). *The Problem of Perception*. Retrieved from Stanford Encyclopedia of Philosophy: http://plato.stanford.edu/entries/perception-problem/
Darwin, C., & Darwin, F. (1880). *The Power of Movement of Plants*. London: John Murray.
Dretske, F. (1989). *Explaining Behavior*. Cambridge, MA: MIT Press.
Goldstein, E. B. (2009). *Sensation and Perception* (8th ed.). New York: Wadsworth.
Hume, D. (1739/1985). *A Treatise of Human Nature*. New York: Penguin.

52   *Perceiving*

Kallmeyer, J., Pockalny, R., Adhikari, R. R., Smith, D. C., & D'Hondt, S. (2012). Global Distribution of Microbial Abundance and in Subseafloor Sediment. *Proceedings of the National Academy of Sciences, 109*(40), 16213–16216.

Keller, D. (2011). *The Restless Plant*. Cambridge, MA: Cambridge University Press.

Knight, T. (1806). On the Direction of the Radicle and Germen During the Vegetation of Seeds. *Philosophical Transactions of the Royal Society of London, 96*, 99–108.

Lucas, S., & Luo, Z. (1993). Adelobasileus From the Upper Triassic of Sest Texas. *Journal of Vertubrate Paleontology, 309*–334.

Margulis, L. (1967). On the Origin of Mitosing Cells. *Journal of Theoretical Biology, 14*(3), 255–274.

Margulis, L. (1981). *Symbiosis in Cell Evolution*. New York: W.H. Freeman.

Millikan, R. (1984). *Language, Thought and Other Biological Categories*. Cambridge, MA: MIT Press.

Morton, A. (1981). *History of Botanical Science*. Orlando, FL: Academic Press.

Noe, A. (2004). *Action in Perception*. Cambridge, MA: MIT Press.

Palmer, S. (1999). *Vision Science*. Cambridge, MA: MIT Press.

Pavlov, I. (1928). *Lectures on Conditioned Reflexes* (W. Gantt, Trans.). London: Allen and Unwin.

Scott, P. (2008). *Physiology and Behavior of Plants*. Hoboken, NJ: Wiley & Sons.

Shettleworth, S. (2009). *Cognition, Evolution, and Behavior* (2nd ed.). New York: Oxford University Press.

Siegel, S. (2010, July 19). *The Contents of Perception*. Retrieved from Stanford Encylopedia of Philosophy: http://plato.stanford.edu/entries/perception-contents/

Sokolowski, R. (1999). *Introduction to Phenomenology*. New York: Cambridge University Press.

Sternberg, R. (2008). *Cognitive Psychology* (5th ed.). Belmont, CA: Wadsworth.

Thompson, E., & Zahavi, D. (2007). Phenomenology. In P. D. Zelazo, M. Moscovitch, & E. Thompson (Eds.), *The Cambridge Handbook on Consciousness*. New York: Cambridge University Press.

Tolman, E. (1948). Cognitive Maps in Rats and Men. *Psychological Review, 55*(4), 189–208.

Whippo, C. W., & Hangarter, R. P. (2006). Phototropism: Bending towards Enlightenment. *The Plant Cell, 18*, 1110–1119.

Whippo, C. W., & Hangarter, R. P. (2009). The 'Sensational' Power of Movement in Plants. *American Journal of Botany, 96*(12), 2115–2127.

Whitman, W. B., Coleman, D. C., & Wiebe, W. J. (1998). Prokaryotes: The Unseen Majority. *Proceedings of the National Academy of Sciences, 95*, 6578–6583.

Zimbardo, P., Johnson, R. L., & Hamilton, V. M. (2011). *Pscyhology: Core Concepts* (7th ed.). New York: Pearson.

3   Feeling

1. How Does it Feel to be a Flytrap?

Imagine you are a Venus flytrap. You dwell in your native territory, North Carolina, in the Green Swamp Preserve (Figure 3.1). It is July. 9 a.m. 84 degrees Fahrenheit and 85% humidity. You are seven years old. Longleaf pines tower above you. The understory is bathed in sunlight. Wiregrass, ferns, and other traps surround you. Your seven leaves lie close to the ground. At the end of each, a pair of reddish lobes lies open, each rimmed with more than a dozen cilia. Several centimeters above your leaves, atop a stem, your two white flowers wobble in a gentle breeze. A bee lands on one. In the acidic and nitrogen-poor soil, your roots are relatively still. Above ground, an ant wanders along the rim of one lobe, creeping onto its surface, brushing one hair there, and then another. Rapidly, the lobe and its mate fold together, the cilia along their rims interlocking like stringy fingers, trapping the ant inside. You begin to secrete enzymes, which eventually allow you to get energy and nutrients from the ant—as well as nitrogen, which you need to build protein.

How does it feel? What is it like?

The bright sun. The warmth. The humidity. The bee on your flower. The breeze. The ant crawling on the lobe of your leaf. Your lobes folding together.

Maybe you find it hard to say. Several people have vividly imagined and portrayed plants coming to life. Audrey II in *The Little Shop of Horrors* has a voracious appetite, for human blood. She also talks, and sings.

Talking of plants 'coming to life' sounds confused, since they're already alive. Still, you may be tempted to talk that way, which might be a symptom of how we tend to think about plants—as not alive, or lifeless. That is very curious, since in 1944 Fritz Heider and Marianna Simmel showed that we tend to attribute agency, mindedness, or life to mere moving shapes, like circles and triangles. So long as they move in certain ways, onlookers describe them as wanting, thinking, and trying.[1] Maybe, then, you find it

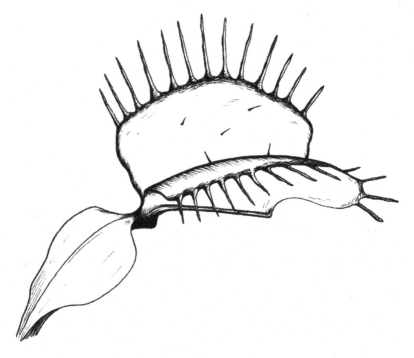

Figure 3.1 Venus flytrap (*Dionaea muscipula*)

hard to see plants as alive because they don't seem to move. And maybe you find it hard to imagine what it's like to be one of them, because you find it hard to see them as alive.

The plants that 'come to life' in stories are clearly not normal plants. Even if we can get inside of Audrey II, understanding her motives or personality, we aren't learning about what goes on for a normal plant. It's more likely that we're simply imagining how it feels to be a human that appears outwardly like a plant.

Try this: act like a tree.

What did you do? Stand up? Raise your arms, making a rough 'Y' or 'Ψ' with your body? Keep really still? That's what I would do. And how would it feel to remain that way? Boring? Tiring? Stifling? Peaceful?

When I imagine being a Venus flytrap, I imagine sitting still in the grass on that warm, humid, summer morning. But that's not right. I'm supposed to be imagining how it feels for the trap, not how I would feel if I were in the same spot as it. It should be more like imagining how a person very, very different from me—anatomically, psychologically, sociologically—feels in some circumstance. For me, that might be like imagining a young woman giving birth in 9263 B.C.E. But that really isn't much closer to imagining how it feels to be a Venus flytrap. Although she and her circumstance are much different from me and mine, I can reasonably imagine that she would be in physical pain, probably afraid, and maybe eager or hopeful. Imagining how a plant feels requires imagining the circumstance of an utterly different sort of organism. Alive, yes. But with a vastly different anatomy and physiology. (And different plants, of course, have very different bodies.)

My attempts to imagine how it feels to be a plant sputter to nothing, which makes me wonder whether it really feels any way at all.

Do plants feel?

2. What Happens in Trapping?

The trapping of a Venus flytrap (*Dionaea muscipula*) is a case of thigmomorphism, a term coined by Mark Jaffe in 1973.[2] Thigmomorphism is simply a change of shape or form in response to touch, or a mechanical stimulus, which includes not just insects, but also other plants, rocks, or wind.[3] Because trapping is not affected by the direction of the stimulus, it is not a tropism, like phototropism or gravitropism. Instead, it is a *nastic* movement—a movement that has no particular direction relative to its stimulus. Hence: thigmonasty (also sometimes called 'seismonasty'). Unlike phototropism and gravitropism, trapping is *reversible*—it can be undone—and does not count as growth, which is typically irreversible.

Another impressive example of thigmomorphism is the Sensitive Plant (*Mimosa pudica*), also known as the Sleeping Plant and the Touch-Me-Not (Figure 3.2). It has compound leaves: on each petiole (leaf stem), there are numerous leaflets (smaller blades), opposite to each other. When the plant is touched in any given spot, the leaflets in the vicinity successively fold inward, in less than a second, about the speed of Venus's trap.

In both the Venus flytrap and the Sensitive Plant, the rapid action is controlled by the pulvinus, a collection of cells at the base of the lobes or leaflets. When these plants are touched, the cells of the pulvinus rapidly lose water, hence turgor, the internal pressure due to water within the cells. They 'deflate.' Water is drawn out of the cells by an increase in sugar in the space outside the cells, coming from the phloem. Plant biologists are still studying precisely how this process happens so quickly.[4]

Thigmomorphism is, in fact, more common than the rarity of the flytrap and the Sensitive Plant might suggest. Stems of bean plants, for instance, thicken in response to sustained exposure to wind or other physical contact.[5] And there are lots of climbing plants that rely on thigmotropism. They grow in the direction of contact, which enables them to wrap around

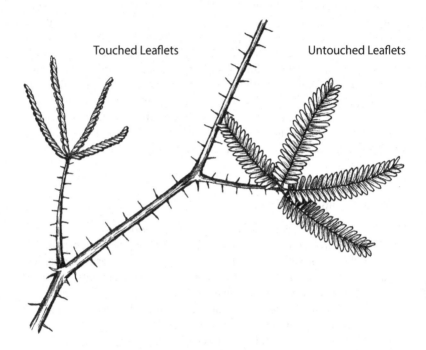

Touched Leaflets   Untouched Leaflets

Figure 3.2 Touch-Me-Not (*Mimosa pudica*)

objects. Roots, too, are thigmotropic, but negatively; they grow away from the direction of the stimulus, which is effectively a way of avoiding physical impediments.[6]

Plants are responsive to various things that affect them throughout a normal day, so there are a variety of 'feelings' they might have, if they feel anything at all. How it feels for a Venus flytrap to trap an ant is just one vivid case. But there is something very special about thigmonasty: it can be significantly dampened by ether![7] Traditionally, ether is a general anesthetic for humans, used to make us unconscious, knocking us out. Since it disables our ability to feel, does it also disable plants' ability to feel?

What do we mean by 'feel'?

3. Qualia

Different things feel different to us. In Chapter Two, we took stock of things that we perceive. I said:

> To my right I see a cup, sitting on a brown desk. It's green, shiny, cylindrical. Voices I hear from behind me, from another room. Inhaling

deeply, I smell coffee, toothpaste, shampoo, and humidity. Toothpaste lingers in my mouth. Placing my hand on my leg, I feel warmth, and the modestly coarse texture of my jeans. My chair pushes against my back and butt.

Not only do I detect these various things, but each has a feel. The cup has a look; the coffee a smell; the toothpaste a taste; the jeans a feel. Each has a distinctive character or quality. The smell of coffee, for instance, differs from, say, the smell of ammonia, and from being told that there is coffee nearby. Our lives are filled with this stuff: how things feel when I'm walking, riding a bike, or accelerating in a car; hunger; urges to urinate, defecate, or vomit; anger; elation; pains, shooting or throbbing or searing.

Philosophers and psychologists have coined various terms for these 'things': "qualia" (singular: "quale"), "raw feels," "sensa," and "phenomenal consciousness."[8] 'Qualia' is still commonly used, and that's the word I will use.[9] When people wonder whether nonhuman animals, computers, or plants are conscious, they are often asking about qualia.[10] That is, 'qualia' is one word for talking about consciousness or, at least, an aspect of it. Qualia are 'part of' the mind; they occur in the mind; to have or undergo them is to have a mind, or to be in a mental state. However, since it is generally agreed that there are unconscious mental states or processes, like an unconscious fear of failure, it is also generally agreed that not all mental states have a feel.

Thinking about qualia and consciousness is very tricky. Sometimes when people wonder about consciousness, they are wondering more specifically about self-consciousness. 'Self-consciousness' can refer to awareness of oneself in some general way, like thinking that I have a short temper. It also includes thinking about some specific mental state, as when I sit grading my students' essays, but start looking out the window at the wine-red leaves on the Japanese maple below, and then realize that I am doing so. Before that realization, when I was just looking at the leaves, arguably I was just plain conscious, having or undergoing some sort of qualia related to the maple tree, not self-conscious. So, one can be conscious without being self-conscious.[11] One tricky thing is that although we can become aware of qualia, hence self-conscious, we are not normally aware of them in that way; rather, they are just aspects of our encounters with things, our dealings with the world. Sometimes this is put by saying that they are "diaphanous," like a fine mesh veil, something through which we encounter things.[12] So, although we are self-conscious when we think about qualia, that doesn't imply that 'having' qualia requires self-consciousness.

That connects with another tricky aspect of qualia. We each have a special relation to our own. Each knows his or her own in a way that others don't. I can know mine faster than I can know yours. Furthermore, to know yours, it seems I have to infer from evidence, but I don't do that for my own.

For instance, I just know how the green coffee cup looks to me. I suppose that if you were in my position, it would look similarly to you. I could ask you how it looks to you. That would give me (good) evidence of how it does indeed look to you. However, I can know mine by a kind of direct inspection, something like looking at my own mind—or just looking at the cup. Some philosophers take very seriously the possibility that green looks one way to me, and another way to you, maybe the way red looks to me—there could be "inverted qualia"—and we could never know.[13]

Given these things, it is not clear how best to investigate qualia, how things look, smell, taste, sound, feel for a creature, especially creatures other than oneself, human and nonhuman. To know those of other people, we can appeal to analogy: "It's this way for me, and since we're both human, it's probably like this for you too." But that buries the possibility that seeing green is one way for me and another way for you. We can ask each other questions, but that too has limitations, since it requires putting qualia into words, which makes our access to each other's qualia dependent on our linguistic facility—our abilities to comprehend and produce words. Here we might opt instead for non-verbal experiments or investigations—which is presumably how we must proceed with nonhuman animals, and other organisms, like plants. But what sort of experiments should we do? What should we look at? Whole-body responses to stimuli? Images of the brain when presented with stimuli? With that sort of data, it seems we would still need to appeal to analogy: "When I am presented with stimulus S, I do XYZ, and my qualia are like this-and-that; when you are presented with S, you also do XYZ, so your qualia are probably like this-and-that too."

4. Neurons and Plant Neurobiology

Nevertheless, we now have a clearer idea of our topic, qualia. That's what we are wondering whether plants have.

How might we figure that out? It's not as if we are wondering whether plants have bones. For in that case, we could just cut them open and see whether there are any. Qualia don't seem to be like that, so far as we now know. In fact, they don't seem to be anywhere in particular; they don't seem to take up space. (That fact may be the best support for Descartes's belief that a mind is an immaterial, non-extended substance.) If we cut someone open in search of qualia, it's not clear what we would be looking for, or what would fulfill our search.

Could it come to pass that someone else could 'access' my qualia? In just the way that I access mine? That could be a premise for a good movie. Reese learns to access Jake's qualia just as well as he can. Initially, she can do so voluntarily, via a qualia-monitor. But she creates a new device, an implant, that gives her 'access' just like Jake's; she 'just has' his qualia. Has Reese become Jake? Are they one mind in two bodies? That could be fun. Such daydreaming points to what many regard as a serious impediment to studying qualia. In "What Is It Like to Be a Bat?" published in 1974, Thomas Nagel contended that we can't really know what it's like for bats to use their distinctive capacity for echolocation.[14] For Nagel, knowing what it's like necessarily involves a first-person point of view, how things are from the point of view of the bat, the subject of that echolocating activity. But with bats, we have only a third-person point of view, a view of them as objects that engage in echolocation, a view of that behavior from outside, not from inside.[15]

A more indirect approach to studying qualia can thus seem appealing. We can first learn what's going on in us when qualia occur, and then look for similar processes in plants, or bats. The nervous system is a good place to start, since it is centrally involved in all our sensations and actions.

My nervous system is a branching network of bundled cells connecting my brain with my spine, from which they spread to my organs, and into my limbs.[16] The majority of animals—the 'bilaterians,' those with bilaterally symmetrical bodies—including the lowly earthworm, have a nervous system roughly similar to mine, one with a central nerve cord (Figure 3.3). It is involved in virtually everything that occurs in or with me, including seeing, thinking, walking, breathing, digesting, sweating, immune defense, and blood circulation. The bundled nerve cells, or neurons, are paths by which one part of my body can rapidly affect other parts of my body. Afferent neurons are paths by which organs and the body affect the spine and brain. Efferent neurons are paths by which the brain and spine affect the organs and the body. The stereotypical neuron looks like an uprooted plant (Figure 3.4). It has a bulbous cell body. From one side extends a long channel, the axon, which ends with hundreds of numerous smaller branches, the terminals. From the other side extend hundreds of channels, dendrites. Via the axon terminals, the neuron affects other neurons, by releasing chemicals (neurotransmitters) into a gap, a synapse. Via the dendrites, the neuron is affected by other neurons, receiving neurotransmitters from a synapse. Some neurons are enormous, stretching up to three feet, connecting the spine with the big toe. Effects in the nervous system can move quickly because most neurons are exceptionally good at conducting electricity, which propagates along the membrane of the axon in just milliseconds, as sodium and potassium ions move into and out of the cell. Axons are efficient conductors largely because they are insulated (though some are not) by other cells (Schwann cells) that coil around axons.

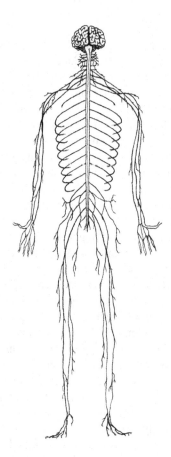

Figure 3.3 Human nervous system

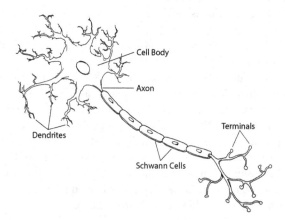

Figure 3.4 Stereotypical motor neuron

Fascinating though nervous systems are, further details might be unnecessary for figuring out whether plants have qualia. For if qualia require a nervous system, then it seems clear that plants don't have qualia, since they don't have a nervous system. Or, anyway, they are not normally regarded as having one— check any botany textbook; you won't find a chapter on their nervous system.[17]

But some botanists have not been so sure. In 2006, in *Trends in Plant Science*, the flagship journal of botany, Eric Brenner and several fellow botanists lobbied for the establishment of "plant neurobiology."[18] Decades before them, Charles and Francis Darwin hypothesized that the roots of a plant are comparable to a brain:

> It is hardly an exaggeration to say that the tip of the radicle thus endowed, and having the power of directing the movements of the adjoining parts, acts like the brain of one of the lower animals; the brain being seated within the anterior end of the body; receiving impressions from the sense organs, and directing the several movements.

Despite having the Darwins on their side, Brenner and his colleagues knew their proposal would shock most of their peers.[19] Since there is a consensus that plants simply do not have neurons, there is nothing for plant *neurobiology* to study. Brenner and his colleagues contended that enough of what plants do—especially the specific processes involved in various tropisms— warranted thinking of plant physiology as significantly analogous to neurophysiology. Their idea was that even if plants do not have cells that are structurally similar to neurons—no cells with dendrites and an axon—they nevertheless engage in activities that are similar to the activities in which neurons engage.[20] Just as a car can operate on electricity and not just gasoline, something can act like a neuron without having the same structure or molecular composition as a typical neuron. In brief, "plant neurobiology" was rooted in the idea that like animals, plants have sophisticated systems for transmitting electrical and chemical signals from one part to another.

You might be tempted to think of xylem and phloem as candidates for plant neurons, but they carry primarily water, nutrients, and sugar, and so are more like an animal's circulatory system—its arteries and veins—than they are like an animal's nervous system. Plant hormones, such as auxin, are not transmitted through xylem and phloem. Rather, they are chemically "pumped" from cell to cell, usually in the tips and along the outer layers of roots and shoots, relying on various intermediary substances.[21] Their movement is much slower than that of an electrical current in an axon: minutes compared to milliseconds. Even relatively fast plant movements, such as those of the Venus flytrap and the Sensitive Plant, are more than ten times slower than the speed at which a neuron acts, tenths of a second compared to thousandths of a second.

That should not be too surprising, since we know plants are much slower than animals. Although seeds and pollen can move from location to location, plants are generally sessile. You might think they lack a rapid response network—a nervous system—because they are sessile. But that cannot be right, for there are sessile *animals*, such as barnacles and corals, and all animals have nervous systems (Figure 3.5). That leaves open the possibility that plants are sessile because they lack a rapid response network. But we should bear in mind that various bacteria are motile (non-sessile), propelled by their flagellum. So, it is not obvious how a plant's sessility relates to its apparent lack of a rapid response network.

Many influential botanists did not like the idea of plant neurobiology, publishing a letter in a subsequent issue of *Trends in Plant Science*, emphatically criticizing it.[22] They wrote, "plant neurobiology does not add to our understanding of plant physiology, plant cell biology or signaling . . .[T]here is no evidence for structures such as neurons, synapses or a brain in plants."[23] Although Brenner and his colleagues initially stood by their contention, they ultimately conceded that a less provocative label for their big ideas would be more appropriate. The Society for Plant Neurobiology became the Society for Plant Signaling and Behavior, publishing the first issue of *Plant Signaling and Behavior* in 2006.[24]

The fact that plants don't have neurons might not matter, since they might not be necessary or sufficient for having qualia.

Brenner's opponents (Alpi and others) seem to be relying on a version of the Identity Theory of Mind—which I introduced in Chapter One. Applied to qualia specifically, the claim would be that neural happenings are necessary

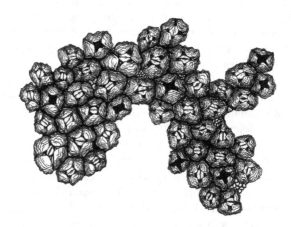

Figure 3.5 Barnacles

and sufficient for qualia. If you have qualia of some sort or other (the smell of coffee, a shooting pain), then your neurons are doing certain things. And vice versa: if your neurons are doing certain things, then you have qualia of some sort or other. That does seem initially plausible, given the correlations we think exist between the nervous system and qualia. But the Identity Theory is saying something more radical than that. It is not saying simply that there is a tight correlation between neuron activity and qualia. It is saying that qualia simply are—they are identical to—some sort of neuron activity. To smell coffee, for instance, simply is for one's neurons to be doing certain things. Smelling coffee is not merely caused by, or correlated with, a certain sort of neuron activity—as if there was the activity and then the qualia. Rather, the claim is that qualia are identical to some neuron activity.[25]

For many philosophers, that is implausible. Maybe there are creatures that have qualia but which have bodies very different from our own—we just haven't found any yet. Analogy: just because we don't know of any bird heavier than the elephant bird, which weighed up to 500 kg, does not imply that there isn't or couldn't be such a bird. Moreover, it can be hard to see why neurons in particular are necessary for qualia. Perhaps something made of different stuff would do just as well. Again, cars can operate on gas or electricity or other forms of power. Perhaps something other than a neuron could play the role of a neuron. (Indeed, that seems to have been what Brenner and his colleagues were saying.) True: all the things that we currently think have qualia—humans, and other mammals—also have neurons. But it does not follow that neurons are necessary for qualia.

If you think it is more likely than not that qualia do require neurons, consider that some philosophers contend that there is a further problem with the Identity Theory of qualia. Whether or not neurons are necessary for qualia, it is not clear why neuron activity is sufficient for qualia. Why should the 'firing' or activation of various neurons amount to feeling anything at all? In *The Conscious Mind*, published in 1996, David Chalmers asks readers to think about zombies.[26] These aren't the slow, dumb, rotting, flesh-eating zombies of *The Walking Dead*. Rather, they are beings that are our exact anatomical duplicates, molecule for molecule. They do everything we do: eat, sleep, sweat, excrete, breathe, walk, talk, go to school, get jobs, have sex, have children, vote in elections, fight wars, throw parties, and on and on. Yet they have no qualia; they 'feel' nothing. Very strange, perhaps, but certainly conceivable, says Chalmers. If so, zombies are at least possible, even if we don't know of any, and even if there really aren't any.

Before Chalmers, in an essay published in 1983, Joseph Levine argued that there is an "explanatory gap" between qualia and physical or biological states or processes.[27] For any physical or biological state or process offered to explain qualia, such as the firing of neurons, one can always wonder why it should feel some way to the organism or system in which it occurs. There would remain a gap in our understanding. According to Chalmers, closing that gap, explaining how a physical or biological state or process could have a feel, is "the hard problem of consciousness."[28]

Chalmers and others stress that the situation with qualia differs from that concerning, say, water. There was a time when, although we were perfectly familiar with water, we didn't know what it was, what it was made of. Eventually, we came to understand that it is a complex molecule, composed of two atoms of hydrogen and one atom of oxygen. Their properties help explain why water behaves as it does: why it freezes and boils at certain temperatures, under certain pressures; why it behaves certain ways as a liquid, why it coheres together, and adheres to other things. Painstaking though the investigations into water have been, there is no 'hard problem' of understanding water; there is no gap between understanding what water is 'made of' and understanding why water does as it does. Not so for qualia, say Chalmers, Levine, and others. It is not even clear what sort of discovery or conceptual advance would allow us to understand why certain physical or biological goings-on should amount to "raw feels." The properties of physical and biological stuff seem so utterly different—different in kind—from the distinctive features of qualia.

Many theorists accept these points but also hold that qualia require or are even identical to *some physical states or other*. To do so, they distinguish between two versions of the Identity Theory.[29] They do so by appealing to a distinction between types and tokens of a type. The word 'tree' has three types of letters: 't,' 'r,' and 'e.' And it has four total tokens, one each of the 't' and 'r' types, and two of the 'e' type. Likewise, a small apple orchard might have just one *type* of tree, but many *tokens* of that type. We have been discussing a *Type*-Identity Theory. It holds that that every token of qualia is identical to a token of one type of physical state or process occurring in neuron. A *Token*-Identity Theory is weaker, holding that each token of qualia is identical to a state or process in *some physical structure or other*. The difference is subtle but important. It is comparable to the difference between holding that footballs need to be made of pigskin, and holding that they must be made of *some appropriate material or other*, including pigskin and rubber.

Given this distinction between *Type-Identity* and *Token-Identity*, we can say that while a Type-Identity Theory is questionable, a Token-Identity Theory remains plausible. So, things that lack neurons, such as plants, might still have qualia, might still feel things.

5. Representations, Again

There are other theories of qualia.

One striking aspect of qualia is that they are often feelings *of* something or other: the smell *of* coffee, the look *of* green, the feel *of* denim, the taste *of* toothpaste, the sound *of* voices, and so on. We sometimes say things like,

"I smell something, but I can't place it." The smell is *of* something. Qualia are not just *of* something in the way that a piece *of* cake is *from* cake. Rather, they are representations *of* something. Thus, for many theorists, qualia seem to be necessarily representational.[30] A representational theory of qualia proposes that qualia are representational states of or episodes in an organism: any state or episode that has a feel is representational, and it has a feel because it is representational.[31]

A representational theory of qualia differs from the Identity Theory because a representational theory is non-committal about what sort of thing, material, or anatomy is necessary or sufficient for having qualia. It can be non-committal about that because it is non-committal about what sort of material or anatomical structure is necessary or sufficient for being in a representational state. Representations can occur in a wide variety of media. Think of how the same image—of, say, a giant sequoia—can appear on the surface of a pond, in a mirror, on a sheet of paper, and in your mind. A representational theory says only that wherever there are qualia, there are representations. By contrast, the Identity Theory says that wherever there are qualia, there are neurons.

According to a representational theory of qualia, plants must have representations if they are to have qualia. In the previous chapter, we found no good evidence for thinking that plants do have representations, states that are representations *of* something. We saw that it is tempting to think plants have representations. For instance, when light from the sun strikes a leaf, the affected part represents the sun or light as being present. Similarly, a branch that sags as a sparrow perches on it represents the presence of something on that branch. As the leaves of a maple wilt on the tenth day of a drought in July, they represent a lack of water. Alas, these examples tacitly rely on the Causal Theory of Representation, which we saw was problematic. Just because Y is caused by X doesn't imply that Y represents X. The sun causes a patch of pavement to get warmer, but the warmness of that patch of pavement does not represent the sun; in general, patches of pavement don't represent anything at all. Likewise, just because the sun affects a photoreceptor in a leaf does not imply that the activity of that photoreceptor represents the sun, or anything else. Causation and representation are not the same thing; effects are not necessarily representations.

If someone wants to convince us that plants have representations, he or she will need a more plausible theory of representation. And a representational theory of qualia supports thinking that plants have qualia only if plants have representations.

But a representational theory of qualia is questionable. Not just anything that represents something else has or undergoes a feel. A drawing of General Sherman, the enormous giant sequoia in Sequoia National Park, is a representation of that tree, but that drawing itself does not have or undergo a feel, nor does the book in which that drawing is printed (Figure 3.6).

Figure 3.6 General Sherman (giant sequoia)

The drawing may look some way to *us*, but that shows only that we have qualia, not the drawing or the book itself. Why should being a representation account for having a feel? The theory plunges into the explanatory gap. It is also questionable that all qualia—or all states or episodes involving qualia—are representational. Pains and moods, such as anxiety, have a feel, but do not obviously represent anything; they're not obviously *of* something. Although a shooting pain in my arm comes *from* my arm, it does not obviously represent my arm or something about my arm, or anything else.[32] Similarly, anxiety need not be *of* or *about* anything; it might just be an inchoate, dreadful feeling. Pains and moods are commonly cited as examples of mental phenomena that are distinct from mental states like beliefs and desires precisely because they seem to be *non-representational*. If that's right, then we can be in a state that has a feel, but which doesn't represent anything. And maybe something similar is true of plants—even if they turn out not to have representational states, perhaps they nevertheless have states that feel certain ways to them.

6. Enactivism

Even if one of these theories that I have briefly discussed were true, neither would likely support thinking that plants have qualia. One requires plants to have neurons; the other requires plants to have representations. It's questionable that they have either. Are there any plausible theories that support thinking that plants feel?

Most theories don't do so. In fact, many theorists take it as just obvious that plants don't have qualia, or consciousness. Here are some representative remarks.

MICHAEL TYE: Consider, for example, the case of plants. There are many different sorts of plant behavior. Some plants climb, others eat flies, still others catapult out seeds. Many plants close their leaves at night. The immediate cause of these activities is something internal to the plants. Seeds are ejected because of the hydration or dehydration of the cell walls in seed pods. Leaves are closed because of water movement in the stems and petioles of the leaves, itself induced by changes in the temperature and light. These inner events or states are surely not phenomenal [i.e., don't involve qualia]. There is nothing it is like to be a Venus Fly Trap or a Morning-Glory.[33]

ROCCO GENNARO: An organism, such as a bat, is conscious if it is able to experience the outer world through its (echo-locatory) senses. There is also something it is like to be a conscious creature whereas there is nothing it is like to be, for example, a table or tree.[34]

KEVIN O'REGAN: Consider a system like our digestive system, the immune system, or plants. One could also look at artificial systems like missile guidance systems or even the lowly thermostat. All these systems could be considered sensorimotor systems. . . . But surely they do not feel anything.[35]

For Gennaro and O'Regan, plants are like missiles and tables; it is just obvious that they don't feel.

How curious! Given that we don't yet know what it is to have qualia, how can informed theorists be so certain that plants don't have them? How can we be certain that they don't feel? There seems to be a conflict. On the one hand, there is no consensus about what is necessary or sufficient for qualia. On the other hand, there is a strong consensus that plants don't have qualia. Tye, Gennaro, and O'Regan—here representing that consensus—seem to think they know more than they do.

More than two millennia ago, Plato recognized this peculiar feature of inquiry. In one famous case, characters in Plato's *Republic* wonder what justice is. They start by listing examples, such as returning a borrowed tool, while injustice includes breaking an agreement. But they remain unsure what justice, in general, is. What is it that makes just things *just*? They try out various definitions, such as: justice is giving what is owed. But they find these definitions inadequate. Now, on what grounds can they find them inadequate? If they know that a certain definition of justice is inadequate, then they must also already know what justice is. How else could they recognize that a definition is inadequate? The general point is put well by Socrates, in Plato's dialogue *Meno*:

> a man cannot search either for what he knows or for what he does not know[.] He cannot search for what he knows—since he knows it, there is no need to search—nor for what he does not know, for he does not know what to look for.[36]

It looks like any inquiry—into justice or qualia—is pointless or impossible. It's pointless if we already know that into which we are inquiring. And if we don't already know, then inquiry is impossible, since we will not be able to recognize an answer if and when we come to it. This predicament has since been called the Paradox of Inquiry. It is a paradox because it seems to prove the opposite of something we think is obvious: that inquiry is possible and has a point.

Of course, it is only natural to think that the Paradox of Inquiry must be mistaken, but it is not easy to say why. One good way to do so appeals to the notion of "reflective equilibrium."[37] Focus on our inquiry into qualia.

We start with at least some knowledge of qualia: for instance, we can point to cases of it (the smell of coffee), and we can point to some creatures (ourselves) that certainly have them. But we hardly know or think we know everything about qualia. For instance, we don't know what it is about us that allows us to have them. That's part of what we want to find out. Our inquiry, then, starts with and is guided by limited and incomplete knowledge. But it only starts there; we seek further knowledge. Often enough, it can turn out that we have to revise or reject things we thought we knew. For instance, as we dig deeper into examples of justice, distinguishing it from other types of good conduct (such as generosity), what initially seemed to be a case of justice might turn out to be characterized better as something else. The same might be true of qualia. In this process, we must decide which of our initial beliefs to keep, and which to revise or abandon in light of new information or new distinctions.

Ultimately, then, it is not utterly bizarre that even in the absence of a consensus about what qualia are, there is a strong consensus that plants don't have them. For the many philosophers (and psychologists, and botanists) who form this consensus, one thing we 'just know' about qualia is that plants and rocks and puddles and tables and missiles don't have them; we just don't yet know why exactly. Confidence in this belief partly expresses a commitment not to give up that belief in the face of further inquiry.

All the same, when the very question is whether plants have qualia, it is tendentious simply to assume that they don't.

ME: Do plants have qualia?
THE CONSENSUS: No.
ME: Oh, why is that?
THE CONSENSUS: They just don't. There's no evidence that they do.
ME: But lack of evidence of qualia doesn't show that they lack qualia. (It's a notorious fallacy to hold otherwise.)
THE CONSENSUS: Well, until we get any such evidence, we are going to proceed as if they don't.
ME: Fine by me, but I still would like to know whether they do.

Furthermore, when inquiring into qualia more generally, it is problematic to start by ruling out the possibility that plants and 'simpler' organisms have qualia, because that makes it hard to think about how anything capable of qualia could have evolved. Did organisms capable of qualia just pop into existence with no relevant precursor? I doubt it. And, just maybe, 'feeling' has something to do with being alive.

There is, however, a relatively new view of mind and consciousness that is not so dismissive of these possibilities: Enactivism. In *Mind in Life*, published in 2007, Evan Thompson provides its most sophisticated articu-lation.[38] Thompson holds that being alive is sufficient for having a mind.[39] Thus, all living things have minds. Thompson claims that to have a mind is, first and foremost, to disclose a world of things that have significance. Here he is drawing on the work of three especially insightful philosophers: Edmund Husserl, Maurice Merleau-Ponty, and Hans Jonas.[40] All are "phenomenologists," thinkers who aim to understand lived human experience, carefully articulating its many varie-ties, structures, and facets.[41]

What is it to "disclose a world of things that have significance"? Focus on the most familiar case of a thing with a mind, a human being, yourself or me. Here at my desk at Dickinson College, in Carlisle, PA, I sit, typing these words on this keyboard, for this chapter, for this book. My green cof-fee cup rests to my right, ready to be sipped. *Mind in Life* is next to it. On my left lies Peter Scott's *Physiology and Plant Behavior*. The wrapper from the granola bar I just finished lies there too, crumbs around it. My small notebook with its 'to do' lists lays open in front of the keyboard. The second movement of John Adams' *Harmonilehre* fills the room.

Here is a world of things that have significance. These items are not just clumps of insignificant matter, made of various periodic elements, obeying various laws of nature, as would be studied by chemists and physicists. No, surrounding me is a network of things that are *for* something, my ongoing project of writing this book. Desk, keyboard, coffee, books, lists, and food have a point or purpose within that project; there are ways they should and should not be used. These things are "disclosed" because they have signifi-cance in virtue of their place in an activity, my project of writing, an activ-ity which in turn has its significance in virtue of its place in several wider contexts: my personal life, my career, contemporary book publishing, and contemporary philosophy. (Some also have roles in other projects. And, of course, there are many other things around me that I haven't mentioned.) Although writing a book is certainly an intellectual activity, that is not the important aspect of the example, that is not what makes it exemplify having a mind. Here, what exemplifies having a mind is the ongoing presence of things that matter through my activity.

Now, given this conception of mind, why exactly does Thompson think that being alive suffices for having a mind?

What exactly is life? What is it to be alive? Biology textbooks commonly say that all living things grow, reproduce, respond to stimuli, metabolize, and maintain homeostasis. Growth is simply to increase (irreversibly) in size (in mass and volume). Reproduction is the ability to create another similar organism, either with or without the involvement of another organ-ism. Responsiveness to stimuli is a capacity to be affected, to change in some way when some condition changes. Metabolism is the set of energy consuming chemical processes that sustain life. In humans, this includes familiar things such as digesting, breathing, and heart-beating. Homeostasis is a condition of stability or constancy. Maintaining it within a system (an organism) requires an ability to monitor and modify internal conditions. Regulating temperature is a simple example. When we get really hot, we sweat. As we cool down, we cease to sweat. If we get chilly from sweating, or because of a breeze, we shiver, warming us up.

Although Thompson accepts these standard claims about life, he stresses a more explanatory conception of life, the theory of autopoiesis developed initially by Humberto Maturana and Francisco Varela.[42] Autopoiesis is simply self-creation. Maturana and Varela thus propose that to be alive is to be self-creating. Living things create themselves, according to the theory, because within them they create and maintain the very structures and processes that are themselves. For Thompson, the paradigm is a single cell, such as a bacterium. The membrane encloses the cytoplasm and the chromosomes, regulating most of what crosses it. Inside the membrane, processes occur that produce that very membrane. Thus, there is a sort of circularity: the membrane enables the ongoing existence of the cytoplasm and chromosomes, which enable the ongoing existence of the membrane, and the cell as a whole[43] (Figure 3.7). For a simple contrast, Thompson offers a car factory, which creates something, but not itself. It produces cars, but they are separate from and independent of the factory. They play no essential part in the factory's ongoing existence (except, perhaps, as a source of money, which can fund the factory).

Thompson adds that living things are not just autopoietic but also "adaptive": they are able to adjust their self-creating processes in response to

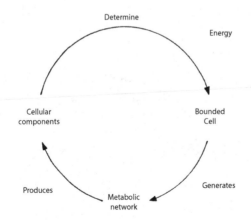

Figure 3.7 A schematic diagram of cellular autopoiesis

changes in their environment, which can be more or less favorable in various ways. He uses "autopoietic" to mean autopoietic-and-adaptive, except where the difference matters, which is what I will do going forward.[44]

We now have the main pieces for understanding Thompson's claim that life suffices for mind. That claim comes to this: autopoiesis suffices for disclosing-a-world-of-significance. Return to the bacterium. By actively creating and maintaining its membrane, it induces an array of things that matter to it in various ways (thus disclosing a world of significance). It exists not in mere space. It is surrounded not merely by value-neutral things with this or that chemical composition, mass, charge, shape, and rigidity. Instead, it has what Jakob von Uexküll (1864–1944) called an "umwelt," a milieu or environment.[45] Some things it actively seeks, or is drawn toward; others it actively avoids. For instance, several types of bacteria survive only in environments that are poor in oxygen; they are obligate anaerobes. Dwelling in the oceans, to find oxygen-poor water, which tends to be distant from the surface, these bacteria rely on magnetotaxis, movement towards or away from a magnetic pole. Inside these bacteria are magnetosomes, chains of magnetite, a naturally magnetic metal[46] (Figure 3.8). In the northern hemisphere, the magnetosome draws the bacteria into deeper water. The direction of geomagnetic north and oxygen *matter* to these bacteria. *Mattering* here needs to be understood in terms of the cell's ongoing self-maintenance and cannot be smoothly assimilated to the 'behavior' of mere rocks, since rocks do not engage in any sort of self-creation or self-maintenance, and nothing 'shows up' to them as to-be-acted-upon in some way or other, as possibilities or opportunities for action. For these reasons, Thompson believes that life suffices for mind.

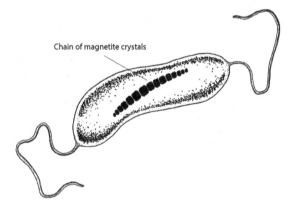

Chain of magnetite crystals

Figure 3.8 Magnetotactic bacterium

Table 3.1 What is a mind?

	What is a mind?	Could plants have minds?
Aristotelianism	Psuche: goal-directed order	Yes
	Nous: intellect or reason	
Mechanism	A type of matter-in-motion	Yes
Cartesian Dualism	A non-bodily entity	No (?)
Darwinism	A suite of abilities of some organisms, resulting from evolution by natural selection	Yes
Behaviorism	Dispositions to behave, which can be gained and lost through habituation	Yes
Identity Theory	The (human?) nervous system	No
Computationalism	A computer	Yes
Enactivism	An autopoietic system	Yes

Return now to qualia. Enactivism holds that qualia (and consciousness more generally) are rooted in the ways in which things matter to an organism, which is rooted in its being an autopoietic and adaptive system. Given all of this, Enactivism implies that for any organism, there is at least a proto-feel to its encounters with things.[47] That includes a Venus flytrap trapping a fly on a warm, humid morning in July. How exactly it feels, we do not know. Surely it is not as robust, complex, or sophisticated as what would be had by humans in that same circumstance—given that our form of life is more variegated and complicated than theirs. Enactivism contends only that these encounters are nevertheless helpfully placed together along a spectrum.

Although Enactivism might be the most promising framework for maintaining that plants feel things, it is definitely a minority view. Despite gaining proponents, it is not even mentioned in several authoritative overviews of qualia and consciousness.[48] For the many theorists who are already sure that plants don't feel things, and aren't conscious, Enactivism's implied support for that idea will simply be a reason to reject Enactivism. However, Enactivism is worthy of further consideration, and in due course we will give it that.

8. Do Plants Feel?

We have seen that many theorists think that plants don't feel. While their theories do provide grounds for believing that, we have also seen that many of these same theorists simply take it for granted—they assume it is true—and craft their theories accordingly. That assumption is unacceptable when the very question is whether plants feel. Among other things, it threatens to leave us in the same bad spot we were in at the end of the last chapter, lumping plants with rocks, puddles, and other non-living things. However, aside from rejecting that assumption, there remains a possibility for distinguishing plants from non-living things: plant responses incorporate and integrate past responses; they remember.

Notes

1 (Heider & Simmel, 1944). For more recent work, see (Scholl & Tremoulet, 2000).
2 (Jaffe, 1973).
3 (Jaffe, 1973), (Scott, 2008), and (Whippo & Hangarter, 2009) all suggest that Charles and Francis Darwin were the first to experimentally investigate thigmotropism and thigmonasty.
4 (Scott, 2008) and (Chehab & Braam, 2009).
5 (Jaffe, Telewski, & Cooke, 1984).
6 (Scott, 2008).
7 (Wallace, 1931) and (De Luccia, 2012).
8 The word "qualia" comes from (Lewis, 1929). "Raw feels" comes from (Tolman, 1932), picked up by (Farrell, 1950) and (Feigl, 1958). "Phenomenal consciousness" comes from (Block, 1995). "Sensa" is older, recognized as a technical term in (Merryless, 1938), which cites (Stout, 1923). Philosophers debate whether these terms pick out precisely the same things, e.g., (van Gulick, 2014) and (Lycan, 2006a).
9 For overviews, see (Kind, 2008) and (Tye, 2013).
10 'Consciousness' can refer to different but related things (van Gulick, 2014). States can be conscious, e.g., the pain of a stubbed toe. Creatures can be conscious, e.g., awake. When we say a creature is conscious, it is often conscious *of* something, whereas when we say a pain is conscious, it is not conscious of anything, but instead conscious *to* someone. In the nineteenth century, many researchers used 'consciousness' to refer to the capacity to think or remember, to have a mind at all (Boakes, 1984).
11 Some philosophers contest that general point. See, for instance, (Gennaro, 2005) and (van Gulick, 2014). Lawrence Weiskranz and colleagues have shown experimentally that "blindsight" is possible. They studied individuals with damage to their visual cortex, who are thus unable to see objects before them. When asked to 'guess' whether something was before or whether something had moved, these individuals did better than chance. See, for instance, (Weiskranz, 1986).
12 The phrase comes from (Moore, 1903).
13 (Byrne, 2010).
14 Nagel's contentions in (Nagel, 1974) are anticipated in (Farrell, 1950), which is commonly not cited.
15 This way of using 'inside' and 'outside' is anticipated by (Collingwood, 1946).
16 (Marieb & Hoehn, 2012).
17 However, you can find otherwise careful authors exaggerating. Peter Scott, for instance, says, "auxins can be viewed as the equivalent of the nervous system

Feeling 75

in animals" (Scott, 2008, p. 163). That remark is confusing in part because if auxins were equivalent to anything related to the nervous system, it would not be the whole system, but instead some part of it, most likely neurotransmitters.
18 (Brenner et al., 2006).
19 For helpful discussion of the Darwin's "root-brain hypothesis," see (Baluška, Mancuso, Volkmann, & Barlow, 2009).
20 For further defense of related ideas, see also (Calvo & Keijzer, 2011).
21 (Scott, 2008).
22 (Alpi, 2007).
23 (Alpi, 2007, pp. 135–136).
24 (Brenner, Stahlberg, Mancuso, Baluška, & Volkenburgh, 2007). For an enjoyable telling of the story, see (Pollan, 2013).
25 For example, (Crick, 1994).
26 (Chalmers, 1996).
27 (Levine, 1983). For a related seminal argument concerning our knowledge of qualia, see (Jackson, 1982), which contends that if you have never seen red, no description of what occurs in seeing red, however thorough it might be, and however intelligent you might be, could convey to you the look of red, what it is like to see red.
28 (Chalmers, 1995). For a philosophical overview, see (Weisberg, 2011).
29 (Smart, 2007).
30 The idea that all conscious states—all states with qualia—are *of* or *directed at* something is centrally important to phenomenology. See, for instance, (Horgan & Tienson, 2002) and (Siewert, 2006).
31 For an overview of representational theories of consciousness, see (Lycan, 2006, p. 8).
32 Some contend otherwise, e.g., (Tye, 1990) and (Tye, 1995).
33 (Tye, 2013).
34 (Gennaro, 2005).
35 (O'Regan, 2014).
36 (Plato, 2002, p. 70 (80e)).
37 The phrase "reflective equilibrium" comes from (Rawls, 1971), and has since been put into wide currency by contemporary philosophers.
38 (Thompson, 2007). For a synopsis, see (Thompson, 2011). In this book, Thompson is building on earlier work done with Francisco Varela and Eleanor Rosch, (Varela, Thompson, & Rosch, 1991).
39 The idea that mind is continuous with life is also known as the Strong Continuity Thesis. See, for instance, (Godfrey-Smith, 1994) and (Godfrey-Smith, 1996). That is my topic in Chapter Six.
40 (Husserl, 1900/1901/2002), (Husserl, 1913), (Merleau-Ponty, 1942/1963), and (Jonas, 1966). In arguing for minimal cognition in plants, Calvo and Keijzer don't address Thompson or Husserl or Merleau-Ponty, but they do acknowledge Jonas (Calvo & Keijzer, 2011).
41 For overviews, see (Thompson & Zahavi, 2007) and (Sokolowski, 1999).
42 (Maturana & Varela, 1972/1980). Thompson says that the standard conception of life merely describes features of living things, but does not explain what makes something count as alive (Thompson, 2007, p. 96).
43 (Thompson, 2007, p. 98).
44 (Thompson, 2007, pp. 149, 158).
45 (von Uexküll, 1934/2010).

76   *Feeling*

46 (Blakemore, 1975) and (Lefèvre & Bazylinski, 2013).
47 Thompson himself does not think that autopoiesis-and-adaptivity suffices for having qualia, or for consciousness (Thompson, 2007, pp. 161–162).
48 (Gennaro, 2005), (Kind, 2008), (Tye, 2013), and (van Gulick, 2014).

Works Cited

Alpi, A. (2007). Plant Neurobiology: No Brain, No Gain? *Trends in Plant Science, 12*(4), 135–136.
Baluška, F., Mancuso, S., Volkmann, D., & Barlow, P. (2009). The 'Root-Brain' Hypothesis of Charles and Francis Darwin. *Plant Signalling and Behavior, 4*(12), 1121–1127.
Blakemore, R. (1975). Magnetotactic Bacteria. *Science, 190*(4212), 377–379.
Block, N. (1995). On a Confusion About a Function of Consciousness. *Behavioral and Brain Sciences, 18*(2), 227–287.
Boakes, R. (1984). *From Darwin to Behaviourism.* New York: Cambridge University Press.
Brenner, E., Stahlberg, R., Mancuso, S., Baluška, F., & Volkenburgh, E. V. (2007). Response to Alpi et al.: Plant Neurobiology: The Gain Is More Than the Name. *Trends in Plant Science, 12*(6), 231–233.
Brenner, E., Stahlberg, R., Mancuso, S., Vivanco, J., Baluška, F., & Van Volkenburgh, E. (2006). Plant Neurobiology: An Integrated View of Plant Signaling. *Trends in Plant Science, 11*(8), 413–419.
Byrne, A. (2010, January 20). *Inverted Qualia.* Retrieved from Stanford Encyclopedia of Philosophy: http://plato.stanford.edu/entries/qualia-inverted/
Calvo, P., & Keijzer, F. (2011). Plants: Adaptive Behavior, Root-Brains, and Minimal Cognition. *Adaptive Behavior, 19*(3), 155–171.
Chalmers, D. (1995). Facing Up to the Problem of Consciousness. *Journal of Consciousness Studies, 2*(3), 200–219.
Chalmers, D. (1996). *The Conscious Mind.* New York: Oxford University Press.
Chehab, E., & Braam, J. (2009). Thigmomorphogenesis: A Complex Plant Response to Mechano-Stimulation. *Journal of Experimental Botany, 60*(1), 43–56.
Collingwood, R. (1946). *The Idea of History.* Oxford: Clarendon.
Crick, F. (1994). *The Astonishing Hypothesis.* New York: Scribners.
De Luccia, T. (2012). Mimosa piduca, Dionaea muscipula and Anesthetics. *Plant Signaling and Behavior, 7*(9), 1163–1167.
Farrell, B. (1950). Experience. *Mind, 59,* 170–198.
Feigl, H. (1958). The 'Mental' and the 'Physical'. In H. Feigl, M. Scriven, & G. Maxwell (Eds.), *Minnesota Studies in the Philosophy of Science* (Vol. II, pp. 370–497). Minneapolis: University of Minnesota.
Gennaro, R. (2005). *Consciousness.* Retrieved from Internet Encyclopedia of Philosophy: www.iep.utm.edu/consciou/
Godfrey-Smith, P. (1994). Spencer and Dewey on Life and Mind. In R. Brooks, & P. Maes (Eds.), *Artificial Life IV: Proceedings of the Fourth International Workshop on the Synthesis and Simulation of Living Systems.* Cambridge, MA: MIT Press.
Godfrey-Smith, P. (1996). *Complexity and the Function of Mind in Nature.* New York: Cambridge University Press.

Heider, F., & Simmel, M. (1944). An Experimental Study of Apparent Behavior. *The American Journal of Psychology, 57*(2), 243–259.

Horgan, T., & Tienson, J. (2002). The Intentionality of Phenomenology and the Phenomenology of Intentionality. In D. Chalmers (Ed.), *Philosophy of Mind: Classical and Contemporary Readings.* New York: Oxford University Press.

Husserl, E. (1900/1901/2002). *Logical Investigations* (J. Findlay, Trans.). New York: Routledge.

Husserl, E. (1913). *Ideas* (W. B. Gibson, Trans.). New York: Routledge.

Jackson, F. (1982). Epiphenomenal Qualia. *Philosophical Quarterly, 32*(127), 127–136.

Jaffe, M. (1973). Thigmomorphogenesis: The Response of Plant Growth and Development to Mechanical Stimulation. *Planta, 114,* 143–157.

Jaffe, M., Telewski, F., & Cooke, P. (1984). Thigmomorphogenesis: On the Mechanical Properties of Mechanically Perturbed Bean Plants. *Plant Physiology, 62,* 73–78.

Jonas, H. (1966). *The Phenomenon of Life: Toward a Philosophical Biology.* New York: Harper & Row.

Kind, A. (2008). *Qualia.* Retrieved from Internet Encyclopedia of Philosophy: www.iep.utm.edu/qualia/

Lefèvre, C., & Bazylinski, D. (2013). Ecology, Diversity, and Evolution of Magnetotactic Bacteria. *Microbiolology and Molecular Biology Reviews, 77*(3), 497–526.

Levine, J. (1983). Materialism and Qualia: The Explanatory Gap. *Pacific Philosophical Quarterly, 64,* 354–361.

Lewis, C. (1929). *Mind and the World Order.* New York: Scribner's.

Lycan, W. (2006a). Consciousness and Qualia Can Be Reduced. In *Contemporary Debates in Cognitive Science* (pp. 189–201). New York: Blackwell.

Lycan, W. (2006b, October 9). *Representational Theories of Consciousness.* Retrieved from Stanford Encyclopedia of Philosophy: http://plato.stanford.edu/entries/consciousness-representational/

Marieb, E., & Hoehn, K. (2012). *Human Anatomy and Physiology* (9th ed.). New York: Pearson.

Maturana, H., & Varela, F. (1972/1980). *Autopoiesis and Cognition.* Dordrecht: Reidel.

Merleau-Ponty, M. (1942/1963). *The Structure of Behavior* (A. Fisher, Trans.). Boston: Beacon.

Merryless, W. (1938). The Status of Sensa. *Australasian Journal of Psychology and Philosophy, 16*(1), 41–59.

Moore, G. (1903). Refutation of Idealism. *Mind, 12*(48), 433–453.

Nagel, T. (1974). What Is It Like to Be a Bat? *Philosophical Review, 83*(4), 435–456.

O'Regan, K. (2014). The Explanatory Status of the Sensorimotor Approach to Phenomenal Consciousness, and Its Appeal to Cognition. *Contemporary Sensorimotor Theory, 15,* 22–35.

Plato. (2002). *Five Dialogues: Euthyphro, Apology, Crito, Meno, Phaedo* (2nd ed., G. Grube, Trans.). Indianapolis, IN: Hackett.

Pollan, M. (2013, December 23). The Intelligent Plant. *New Yorker.*

Rawls, J. (1971). *A Theory of Justice.* Cambridge, MA: Harvard University Press.

Scholl, B., & Tremoulet, P. (2000). Perceptual Causality and Animacy. *Trends in Cognitive Science, 4*(8), 299–309.

Scott, P. (2008). *Physiology and Behavior of Plants.* Hoboken, NJ: Wiley & Sons.

Siewert, C. (2006, December 23). *Consciousness and Intentionality.* Retrieved from Stanford Encyclopedia of Philosophy: http://plato.stanford.edu/entries/consciousness-intentionality/

Smart, J. (2007, May 18). *The Mind/Brain Identity Theory.* Retrieved from Stanford Encyclopedia of Philosophy: http://plato.stanford.edu/entries/mind-identity/

Sokolowski, R. (1999). *Introduction to Phenomenology.* New York: Cambridge University Press.

Stout, G. (1923). Prof. Alexander's Theory of Sense Perception. *Mind, 31*(124), 385–412.

Thompson, E. (2007). *Mind in Life.* Cambridge, MA: Belknap.

Thompson, E. (2011). Precis of Mind in Life. *Journal of Consciousness Studies, 18*(5–6), 10–22.

Thompson, E., & Zahavi, D. (2007). Phenomenology. In P. D. Zelazo, M. Moscovitch, & E. Thompson (Eds.), *The Cambridge Handbook on Consciousness.* New York: Cambridge University Press.

Tolman, E. (1932). *Purposive Behavior in Animals and Men.* Berkeley, CA: University of California.

Tye, M. (1990). A Representational Theory of Pains and Their Phenomenal Character. In J. Tomberlin (Ed.), *Philosophical Perspectives* (Vol. 9). Atascadero, CA: Ridgeview.

Tye, M. (1995). *Ten Problems of Consciousness.* Cambridge, MA: MIT Press.

Tye, M. (2013, April 22). *Qualia.* Retrieved from Stanford Encyclopedia of Philosophy: http://plato.stanford.edu/entries/qualia/

van Gulick, R. (2014, January 14). *Consciousness.* Retrieved from Stanford Encyclopedia of Philosophy: http://plato.stanford.edu/entries/consciousness/

Varela, F. J., Thompson, E., & Rosch, E. (1991). *The Embodied Mind: Cognitive Science and Human Experience.* Cambridge, MA: MIT Press.

von Uexküll, J. (1934/2010). *A Foray Into the Worlds of Animals and Men* (J. O'Neil, Trans.). Minneapolis: Universy of Minnesota Press.

Wallace, R. (1931). Studies of the Sensitivity of Mimosa Piduca, II: The Effect of Animal Anesthetics and Certain Compounds Upon Seismonic Activity. *American Journal of Botany, 18*(3), 215–235.

Weisberg, J. (2011). *The Hard Problem of Consciousness.* Retrieved from Internet Encyclopedia of Philosophy: www.iep.utm.edu/hard-con/

Weiskranz, L. (1986). *Blindsight: A Case Study and Implications.* New York: Oxford University Press.

Whippo, C. W., & Hangarter, R. P. (2009). The 'Sensational' Power of Movement in Plants. *American Journal of Botany, 96*(12), 2115–2127.

4 Remembering

1. Remembering Plants

Only when two of its hairs are touched does the Venus flytrap close (Figure 4.1). The second need not be touched immediately after the first, but it must be touched within twenty seconds of the first. Botanists conjecture that the trap uses *two* triggers because it helps avoid wasting energy on closing and re-opening when there is nothing of nutritional value present, such as dead leaf debris. With two triggers, the chances are better that there is something moving in the trap. By restricting the time in which the second hair can be touched, the chances are better still. Otherwise, two pieces of dead leaf debris, landing many minutes apart, could get the trap to shut. These aspects of trapping suggest that the plant is somehow able to remember that one hair has recently been touched.[1]

Consider also root growth, which, as I mentioned earlier, integrates gravitropism and thigmotropism (and hydrotropism, too). Roots will grow downward unless they are mechanically impeded, which causes them to begin growing sideways, perpendicular to the previous direction of growth. After a short time, the root will resume growing downward. If it is again impeded, it will return to horizontal growth. This behavior suggests the plant or the root somehow remembers that it was recently impeded, or that it has been growing horizontally for a length of time, and so can try again to grow downward.[2]

Photoperiodism is another apparent case of plants remembering. Photoperiodism is growth (particularly flowering) in response to the amount of light to which the plant has been exposed. Photoperiodism takes three different forms. Some plants flower only when days are long; thus, they flower in the spring or summer; they are "long-day" plants. "Short-day" plants flower only when days are short, hence in the fall or winter. And still others are neutral, preferring neither short nor long days for flowering. To be either short-day or long-day, it seems plants must somehow remember how much light they have encountered[3] (Figure 4.2).

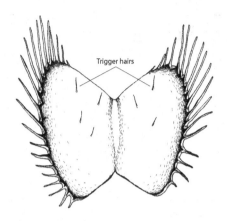

Figure 4.1 Trigger hairs of a Venus flytrap

Figure 4.2 A long-day plant, the carnation (*Dianthus caryophyllus*)

If plants can remember in these ways, they can also learn. And most seem to. Young bean plants, for instance, acclimate to windy conditions by growing thicker stems, thicker than siblings not grown in such conditions. When exposed to the windier conditions, these siblings get blown over. Not all bean plants grow in precisely the same way, but instead are (phenotypically) "plastic," appearing to learn and adjust to their conditions.[4]

Thus, it is very tempting to say that plants have memory; they learn and remember. Do they? What exactly is remembering anyway?

2. What Is Memory?

On this average morning, among many other things, I remembered:

how to walk
how to type
how to find music on YouTube
the names of our cats
the haunting scene from last night's episode of *The Walking Dead*
the year Wu-Tang's first album came out
that many people love rap, but many others don't
what rap is
what people are
to chew my cereal before swallowing
to put on my coat before leaving

That list is just a small sample of many things I remember. But it indicates how thoroughly we depend on memory. So thorough is our dependence that it's easy to overlook, as if remembering was only something we intermittently do, on tests, when procrastinating from work, or practicing a new skill.

All memories are ways in which the past influences the present. Some memories seem to take us away from the present, or to bring the past-and-gone into the present. Memory makes possible love and friendship, but also fear and regret, animosity and war. Alzheimer's disease painfully suggests that memory has something to do with our very identities, our tendency to be one-and-the-same person from one week to the next. If my memory is significantly disabled, it can seem to others that *I* have ceased to be, replaced by a look-alike.

Over the past century, among psychologists a consensus has emerged that there are different categories of memory.[5] Remembering specific events—such as my memory of a scene from a show I watched last night—is *episodic* memory. Remembering facts, specific or general—such as the year a certain album was released—is *semantic* or *factual* memory. Remembering how to do things—such as my remembering how to find a song on You-Tube—is *procedural* or *skill* memory. Procedural memory is thought to differ from episodic and semantic memory, because unlike them, it does not aim at an accurate portrayal of how things are or were, a fact or an event. Instead, it is closer to a portrayal of how things should be or become, how one's body should move or be positioned.

All three types of memory are thought to involve the encoding, storage, and retrieval of information.[6] An episode is undergone; a fact is heard; a procedure is performed; each is encoded. Then it is stored, and retrieved in some subsequent circumstance or eliciting condition. Each type of memory (episodes, facts, skills) might be available for only a short time, or it can be available for a much longer time. Many of us will remember how to tie our shoes until we're dead. And we will remember that humans are animals for just as long. But nearly all of us have already forgotten the exact words of the first sentence of this paragraph. After hearing a song on the radio, many of us can hum the melody shortly thereafter, but cannot reproduce it later that same day, nor even hear it in our mind's ear.

Memory and learning are closely related.[7] Learning is necessary for memory. To remember that Wu-Tang's first album came out in 1993, I must first learn that fact. To remember how to find music on YouTube, I must first learn how to do it. Thus, learning appears to correspond at least to the encoding and storage of facts and skills. Arguably it also includes their retrieval, since one has not learned something if one can never recall or reproduce it. And memory is necessary for learning. To learn a fact or a skill, you must at least be able to store it, which implies that you must have encoded it. All that suggests that memory and learning refer to overlapping phenomena.

Simple learning—simple conditioning and habituation—pervades the animal kingdom. Pavlov's dogs exemplify simple conditioning.[8] They initially salivated upon seeing food. Then, on several occasions, a bell tone accompanied the presentation of food. Subsequently, the dogs salivated upon hearing the bell tone alone, in the absence of the food. They had been "conditioned" to "associate" the bell tone with food. Habituation is illustrated well by the hamsters I mentioned in Chapter Two. Upon initially encountering another's scent, a hamster will vigorously sniff it, but over time does so less vigorously. It habituates to the scent. When it encounters a new scent, again it sniffs vigorously, dishabituating from less vigorous sniffing. Dogs and hamsters are sophisticated mammals, but even fruit flies (*Drosophila melanogaster*), creatures so small they fit through the tiny mesh of a typical screen door, exhibit these behaviors[9] (Figure 4.3). The point is

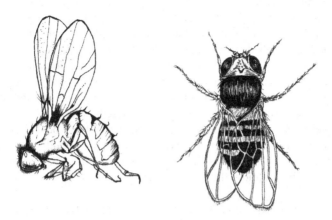

Figure 4.3 Fruit fly (*Drosophila melanogaster*)

this: to the extent that all learning involves memory, and many 'simple' creatures exhibit conditioning and habituation, those creatures remember. Simple learning and memory pervade the animal kingdom.

Can we find them in the *plant* kingdom?

3. Do Plants Remember?

Think back to the potential cases of plant memory that I mentioned at the start: the flytrap's two trigger hairs; the integration of gravitropism and thigmotropism in roots; photoperiodism; and stem thickening in response to a windy environment. Do any of these involve episodic, semantic, or procedural memory?

None seems to involve episodic memory. Think about the flytrap. We have no reason to believe that when the second hair is touched, the plant 'envisions' the touching of the first hair.

None seems like procedural memory, either. When the second hair of the flytrap is touched, and the lobes fold together, that is something the plant does, a 'procedure' it goes through, but we have no reason to think that this is something the plant remembers rather than something the plant simply can do. Blinking in response to a puff of air (during a glaucoma test) is something that you do, but it isn't something you remember how to do, like using garden shears. Unlike simply having a tendency to do something in certain circumstances, remembering how to do something requires being unable initially to do it, and becoming able to do it.

A bit more plausible is that these plant behaviors involve semantic or factual memory, memory of a fact. For instance, although the trap does not envision the touching of its first hair, it might still remember that the first hair has been touched. However, even that is questionable. A piece of granite might crack when struck with a specific force only if it has been previously exposed to a sufficiently low temperature. But that doesn't imply that the granite remembers that it has been exposed to that temperature. Rather, the granite's own temperature simply has been reduced.

However, as Daniel Chamowitz suggests, even if these behaviors do not involve any of the three recognized types of memory—episodic, procedural, semantic—it remains possible that they involve the storage, encoding, and retrieval of information, the common structure of the three categories of memory.

In addition to those already mentioned, a great variety of plant behaviors do seem to fit that description.

Consider vernalization, the ability of many plants to flower only if exposed to a prolonged period of cold.[10] Most of us know that a great many plants produce flowers only in the spring. Isn't that just because they need warmer temperatures and more light? No, it's not, Trofim Lysenko discovered in 1928. He found that these plants—he studied wheat, specifically—must also be exposed to a period of cold before they commence flowering. This keeps the plant from flowering too soon, on an unseasonably warm day, which would be wasted energy if the cold immediately returned, killing the flowers. As with photoperiodism, this suggests that plants store information about how long they have been exposed to a low temperature.

Also, we have seen that many plants are phototropic: they grow towards the sun, or a light source. Photo*torsion* is the related capacity to turn or twist towards the sun. Leaves of many plants do this. Over the course of a day, as the sun moves across the sky, these leaves turn with it, towards it. As Paco Calvo has pointed out, the neat thing, the memory-like thing, is that overnight, the leaves turn back to where the sun will be in the morning![11] They seem to remember where the sun was, or how their leaves were oriented many hours earlier. The basic hypothesis is that they have an internal clock—a circadian clock—an internal device or process that tracks a pattern in their environment.

A shoot that has been growing horizontally—perhaps because it has been knocked over, or mechanically impeded—will begin growing vertically, but it will overshoot the vertical position, and then eventually grow back towards it. Vertical seems to be the shoot's goal, and the shoot seems to be able to check whether it has reached that goal. Roots do this too; they oscillate; they grow past one orientation, only to grow back to that orientation. It is a case of learning and error-correction, depending on stored information, according to Anthony Trewavas.[12] He thinks all acclimation to circumstances, all phenotypic plasticity, requires this sort of thing.

According to Monica Gagliano and her colleagues, the Sensitive Plant (*Mimosa*) appears to habituate to touch. Its leaves cease to fold when repeatedly touched; it gets used to such stimulation.[13] As the stimulation diminishes, the folding response resumes. One hypothesis: the plant stops responding because responding tends to be a waste of energy; there is no need to respond. If true, Sensitive Plants grown in circumstances in which mechanical perturbation does not correlate with any threat to the plant will habituate more quickly than plants grown in other circumstances. And that is indeed what Gagliano and her colleagues have found.

Several sorts of behaviors suggest that plants encode, store, and retrieve information. To test that suggestion, we should look more closely at information.

4. Information

We live in the information age, entangled in information networks, daily riding the information superhighway, intermittently stalled and irritated by information bottlenecks, constantly reminded that information is power, indeed money, and, conversely, afraid that our personal information is not secure.

Talk of information is ubiquitous, which can lull us into thinking that we know what it is. But 'information' refers to many different things: videos, pictures, music, maps, news articles, fossils, spreadsheets, blueprints, fingerprints, blood tests, and genetic sequences. What they have in common, or even that they have anything in common, is not obvious.

Psychologists don't always linger over what they mean when they say that memory necessarily involves encoding, storing, and retrieving information. And, as it turns out, they could mean very different things, connecting with our earlier discussion of representations.

Following various contemporary theorists, we can distinguish two sorts of information. The first sort is illustrated by radio waves and bird tracks. A particular state of a radio wave (the signal) correlates with and so carries information about a particular sound, a song, or a voice (the source). A track in the dirt left by a sparrow (the signal) correlates with and so carries information about that sparrow, its foot (the source) (Figure 4.4). Anything that can be in different states can be a source. A signal that carries information about that source is anything whose states correlate or co-vary with the states of the source, often because of a causal connection between them. The mathematical theory of information ("information theory"), inaugurated by Claude Shannon in 1948, aspires to make these ideas precise, quantifiable, and measurable.[14]

The
Source

The
Signal

Figure 4.4 An example of information. The track (the signal) is caused by and therefore carries information about the bird (the source).

Nearly everything carries this sort of information about something else. Smoke carries information about fire; light carries information about the objects from which it was reflected; tree rings carry information about the age of trees; the length of the day carries information about the angle of the earth relative to the sun; falling barometric pressure carries information about a coming storm; breath carries information about recent alcohol consumption. Our world is saturated with information. Everything is bathed in it. Nearly everything *is* information.

We can call this sort of information 'weak information'; sometimes it is called 'causal information.'

The second sort of information is, in essence, representational, exemplified by sentences of natural languages, such as Arabic or English. The sentence "Dinah is in the kitchen" portrays Dinah as being in the kitchen. It informs us about Dinah, and the kitchen. Or, at least, it purports to. Dinah might not be in the kitchen. The sentence could be false. This sort of information we can call 'strong information.' Sometimes it is called 'semantic information.' It has the possibility of being false, of being about a thing, but portraying it incorrectly, inaccurately, falsely.

Now, you might think that weak information can also be false. For instance, you might have thought that since a correlation between X and

Y implies that X carries information about Y, a lack of correlation between them implies that X carries false information about Y. But that would be a mistake. X carries weak information about Y *only when* the states of X correlate with the states of Y. If and when they don't correlate, X simply doesn't carry weak information about Y; X carries *no* information about Y, not *false* information about it. Weak information cannot be false, thus differing crucially from strong information.

Another way to put it: strong information but not weak information is genuinely representational, capable of misrepresenting things.

Plants certainly encode, store, and retrieve weak information. Nearly everything does. Plants and their parts—their shoots, roots, leaves, cells—*encode* weak information about their environment simply because they correlate with parts of their environment. The production and distribution of auxin in a shoot correlates with the position of the sun. Plants *store* such information about their environment because these correlations persist through time. Often this is because there are chains of information, chains of correlation between something in the environment and one part of a plant, and then between that part and another part. The accumulation of auxin on one side of a shoot correlates with the production of auxin at the tip, which correlates with the position of the sun. When later activities depend on earlier correlations in this way, plants and their parts can also be said to *retrieve* that information. The bending of the shoot draws on the correlation between auxin production and sun position.

So it seems that we can say plants do have a sort of memory, if only a minimal sort, or a precursor. Yet we should take care. Intuitively, remembering requires (1) the leaving of a trace, and (2) the subsequent use (or reproduction) of that trace. The encoding, storing, and retrieval of weak information in plants display (1) and (2). But (1) and (2) don't obviously suffice for remembering. Many things that involve (1) and (2) are not normally taken to be cases of remembering, such as a piece of granite. Prolonged exposure to cold temperature leaves a trace in the granite; it lowers the temperature of the granite. That lower temperature affects the granite's subsequent 'behavior,' whether it cracks when struck. Yet we do not normally think of granite as remembering anything at all, even in a minimal sense. Perhaps, you might say, we have been mistaken, and need to reconsider whether rocks remember. Maybe, I say, but nothing so far compels us to do so, for we can make very good sense of what rocks do by talking simply of causation, correlation, and weak information, never mentioning memory. Similarly, Chamowitz claims that biological inheritance is a sort of remembering, since each generation bears the mark of a preceding generation—many, many preceding generations. But that is not a very good reason to think of inheritance as remembering, for it is like saying that a light bulb remembers that its switch has been flipped because it bears a trace that its switch has been flipped. We should reserve the concepts of memory and remembering for cases where talk of causation and correlation won't do.

That plants encode, store, and retrieve weak information does not give us a very good reason for saying that they remember. More interesting is whether they encode, store, and retrieve *strong* information, whether they form *representations*.

In preceding chapters, we talked about representation, and considered the simple Causal Theory of Representation, but put off looking at other theories. Now is the time to take a further look.

According to one currently influential theory, one thing X represents another thing Y if X's *job* or *function* is to be caused by Y.[15] For instance, a ringing doorbell represents someone pushing the button because the bell's job is to ring in response to a pushing of the button. Normally, the ringing is caused by exactly that. But even when it is caused by something else—a short circuit, for instance—the ringing still represents the button as having been pushed. Of course, in that case, the button has not actually been pushed. The ringing bell thus misrepresents the button as having been pushed. Similar things can be said of organisms, or their parts. This sort of theory looks very appealing because it seems to allow for misrepresentation. Since it emphasizes *jobs* or *functions*, let's call this the Functional Theory of Representation.

The Functional Theory of Representation differs crucially from the Causal Theory of Representation. The Causal Theory holds that anything that has a cause is a representation, but the Functional Theory rejects that. It holds instead that only things that have the job or function of being caused by something else are representations.

To understand the Functional Theory better, and the prospects for strong information or representations in plants, we need to understand functions better.

Table 4.1 Theories of representation

	What is a representation?	*What can be a representation?*
Causal Theory	If X causes Y, then Y represents X.	Anything that has cause
Functional Theory	If Y has the job or function of being caused by X, then Y represents X.	Only things with jobs or functions (to be caused by something else); not just anything that has a cause

5. Functions

Biology textbooks and courses brim with remarks about what organ systems, organs, tissues, cells, and organelles are *for*, what their *functions* or *jobs* are. Physiology is the study of such functions, of what these parts do. A book or course on human physiology tells you that ears are for hearing; eyes are for seeing; hearts are for pumping blood; lungs are for oxygenating blood; white blood cells are for combating infection; and so on. A book or course on plant physiology tells you that xylem is for water transport; leaves are for gas exchange; bark is for protection; chloroplasts are for photosynthesis; and so on. Talk of functions pervades biology.

Although it's common, saying that parts of organisms have jobs or functions can sound odd. Think about human artifacts. The job or function of a mousetrap is to trap mice. The job of a thermostat is to regulate the temperature in a space, such as a room or refrigerator. They have those jobs not simply because they happen to do those things, but in part because we persons give them those jobs. A mousetrap that doesn't or even can't trap any mice is still a mousetrap, a thing whose job is to trap mice. Human artifacts such as these have their jobs bestowed on them by us. The same does not seem true for parts of organisms. We did not bestow, for instance, the job of hearing on ears. And xylem would have been for water transport even if we had never existed.

Until very recently, most philosophers and scientists thought that saying a thing had a job, function, or purpose implied either that it had a mind itself, or that it was designed by something with a mind. For to have a job is to have a goal, and to have a goal is not merely to achieve that goal, but to aim at or be aimed at doing so, which requires a mind. Thus, to say that xylem has the job of transporting water was held to imply that it (or the plant) has a mind, or that it has a designer. Starting in the nineteenth century, however, particularly after Darwin's *Origin of Species* in 1859, such talk started to look suspicious to some. In the light of the theory of evolution by natural selection—the thought went—plants don't have minds or a designer. Some held out hope that such talk could be shown to be harmless. And, indeed, in the past forty years, philosophers have articulated new ways to think about functions.[16]

The human circulatory system circulates blood: the heart pumps, and the arteries and veins convey blood to different parts of the body. Those are their functions, defined in terms of their contribution to circulation. In 1975, Robert Cummins proposed that this strategy of "functional analysis" is a good way to think about functions.[17] A functional analysis starts with some process or ability (circulation), and explains it in terms of the functions of component parts (hearts, arteries, veins). Things have functions relative to a whole system of which they are a part. Plants included. Phototropism is growth towards a light source. How does this process work? As we have seen, photoreceptors on the illuminated side stimulate the production of auxin, which is then distributed to the unilluminated side. The photoreceptors have the function of responding to light. Or consider gravitropism. Roots grow downward because statoliths in amyoplasts 'fall' with the direction of gravity. That is the statoliths' function. This is sometimes called the Systemic View of functions. It allows us to talk of functions, jobs, or purposes without tacitly appealing to a designer.

Ruth Millikan and others have alleged that the Systemic View makes no room for the possibility of malfunctioning.[18] When a heart doesn't pump, blood doesn't circulate. Like Millikan, you might be tempted to say that the heart is not doing its job; it has malfunctioned. According to the Systemic View, however, the heart is not malfunctioning at all, for a heart that isn't pumping also isn't contributing to circulation at all, and so has no function. What might have seemed to you to be malfunction turns out to be, on the Systemic View, a lack of function. In a sense, a seized heart is no longer a heart, but a heart in name alone. The same is true of statoliths: when they don't respond to gravity—as in Knight's experiments—they seem to be malfunctioning. The Systemic View holds, however, that in that case, the statoliths simply do not have the job of contributing to growth in the direction of gravity. So, it seems that on the Systematic View of functions, there is no possibility of malfunction.

Millikan and others think the Systemic View conflates two things: having a *tendency* or *propensity* to do something (such as pumping blood), and having the *function* to do that thing. Better to keep them separate, she thinks. A thing can have a tendency to do something even if doing so is not its function. The sun constantly pulls on the earth, but doing so is not its function or job. And a thing can have a function to do something even if it does not tend to do that thing. A stiff hinge might never let a door swing, but that is still its function. In the biological realm: an eye might be blind, but it is still for seeing. For philosophers like Millikan, talk of functions should be reserved for cases where there is a possibility of malfunction or error.

Along with many other philosophers, Millikan prefers a different conception of functions, one that makes room for the possibility of malfunction. For them, a thing's function is what it has been (naturally) selected for doing. The heart's function is to pump blood, because that is what the heart was *selected for* doing. To say that the heart was selected for pumping is to say that pumping contributed to the relatively higher *fitness* of past organisms with hearts, making those organisms able to reproduce more than other organisms that had hearts that did not pump. Imagine that many millions of years ago, there emerged organisms that had proto-hearts, some of which pumped, others of which did not. Suppose that the ones with pumping proto-hearts lived longer or reproduced just a bit more than those organisms with non-pumping proto-hearts. Supposing that continues, the ones with pumping proto-hearts would come to dominate the population; they would be selected. And their hearts would be selected for pumping, since that is part of the reason those organisms got selected. Thereby, the proto-heart 'acquires' the function of pumping. (From there, further selection would occur, now between different sorts of pumping proto-hearts, leading eventually, over many, many generations to, say, the mammalian heart.) Photoreceptors are similar. Their function is to 'receive' light, for that was what they were selected for doing; their doing so gave organisms with them a fitness advantage over related organisms with quasi-photoreceptors that did not do so. Function is bestowed by selection, without need of a designer, or a knowing, forward-looking selector. Because this view stresses the history or origin of an organ—its etiology—this view is sometimes called the Etiological View of functions.

Unlike the Systemic View, the Etiological View makes room for malfunction. A heart's function is whatever hearts in past organisms did to give those organisms an advantage over others. A thing's function is whatever things of that type did in the past to help organisms with it be fitter than other organisms of the same sort. There can be malfunctions because a thing's function is not necessarily the same as what it actually does. A heart malfunctions when it does not pump, perhaps because of disease, improper development, or malnutrition.

Since it offers a way to make sense of malfunction, the Etiological View tends to seem like the better view. However, it also has some weaknesses. First, without being able to look back in time, how can we know what some process or organ was selected for? And if we can't know that, we can't know what a thing's function is; we would be stuck speculating. Worse, it can seem as if the Etiological View relies on the Systematic View first to discern the function of a thing—what it currently contributes to the operation of the whole organism—and then merely speculates about the evolutionary history that would have bestowed that function on that organ.[19] Second, many practicing biologists—especially those who study the structure and function of parts of organisms, the morphologists and the physiologists—do not appear to figure out the function of things by considering their evolutionary history. Instead, they seem to rely on the Systematic View, asking what contribution a thing actually, currently makes to the operation of a system. For instance, a plant physiologist does not ask how statoliths evolved in order to figure out their function. Rather, the plant physiologist looks at what contribution they currently make to gravitropism. To many practicing biologists, these look like separate issues: how a structure evolved, and what that structure does.[20] So, the Etiological View is not obviously best.

Both views of functions have strengths and weaknesses. Which is right? That is a difficult question. It is not as if we are asking which of two plants is taller, which we could settle by measuring. No, here we are asking about which of two ways of thinking about something (functions) is the better way of thinking about that sort of thing. The truer one, you might want to exclaim. But how should we decide that? We can start by considering how well each conception covers cases. A good view of functions properly sorts things that do and don't have functions: it will count all and only things that have functions as having functions. The Etiological View does somewhat better here, since the Systematic View says that an allegedly malfunctioning heart has no function at all, and that the sun has a function. But other considerations matter too. We should ask about the implications and assumptions of both conceptions. For instance, both avoid assuming there is a supreme designer, which philosophers and scientists tend to count as a virtue. However, the Etiological View implies that we must study evolutionary history to discern the functions of things. That seems to conflict with what successful biologists do, while also making it very difficult to discern a thing's function, since we have only very limited access to the past.

Currently, there is no consensus among theorists on which of these views (or variations of them) is best. Ideally, we could arrive at a conception of function that handles cases well, and meshes well with successful biological practice. Happily, for our purposes here, we don't need to decide between them. What matters is that they are plausible if not perfect ways of understanding how biological items can have functions, even if they don't have a designer.

6. The Functional Theory of Representation

We've been discussing functions because we want to understand better the Functional Theory of Representation, and whether plants have representations (or strong information). We can now clarify that theory. One of the most influential versions of the theory relies on the Etiological View of functions.[21] It contends that X represents Y when X was selected for being caused by Y.[22] A whole lot is compressed into that short claim. Let me unpack it with a good example, gravitropism. The positions of the statoliths represent the direction of gravity because their position was selected for being caused by the direction of gravity. Unpacking that: past plants with statoliths that 'fell' with the direction of gravity were fitter than past plants with statoliths that didn't do that; thus, statoliths were 'selected for'—they acquired the job or function of—moving in the direction of gravity. When Thomas Knight manipulated the position of the statoliths with his wheel, subjecting them to a force other than gravity, that position misrepresented the direction of gravity.

According to the Functional Theory, states of many plant parts represent things. In fact, it was this theory that initially got me wondering about plant minds. That is because many plant parts have the function to be caused by something else. 'Activated' states of photoreceptors represent light, because it's their job to be so affected. Stimulation of Venus's trigger hairs represents the presence of an object on its lobe, because it's their job to be so affected. The Theory is equally striking for implying that even bacteria have representations. Those anaerobic bacteria, the ones that need and seek oxygen-poor water? Their magnetosomes represent the direction of oxygen-poor water (or is it magnetic north?). When the magnetosomes are artificially stimulated by a toy magnet, the magnetosomes misrepresent the direction of oxygen-poor water.

So, if this theory is true, plants do have representations, or strong information.[23] They could be said, then, to encode, store, and retrieve such information when the relevant organ or part is stimulated (encoding), having a further effect on other parts whose job is to be so affected (storing), which in turn affects subsequent behavior (retrieval). If this theory is true, we would also have to revisit our claims about perception and feeling, for it would suggest that plants might indeed be capable of both.

Is the Functional Theory true?

Here is the main issue: Does having the job of being caused by a certain sort of thing count as representing that thing? It can seem so. The position of statoliths in the amyoplasts *seems* to represent the direction of gravity. Think about Knight's experiment on gravitropism. He rotated the plant on a water-propelled wheel. When the plant was rotated, the statoliths in its root tips went with the direction of centrifugal force, not gravity, and the roots started to grow in that direction. The position of the statoliths seems to have misrepresented the direction of gravity.

Think now about your bathroom sink. The job of the valve is to open when the knob is turned. Does the open valve represent that the knob is turned? Does it represent anything at all? The Functional Theory implies that it does, but we don't normally think that the position of the valve represents anything at all. True, a plumber investigating the sink might treat the open valve as a sign of a turned knob, but here the valve works as a representation only because of the plumber's knowledge. Likewise, we can and do use saturated earth as a sign of (recent) rain, but the saturated earth is a sign here only because of our regarding it as such. Consider a biological example. It is the job of my index finger to extend when a nerve impulse reaches it. But the extending of my finger is not in itself a representation of the arrival of such an impulse, or of anything at all. The Functional Theory of Representation looks wrong.

Let me summarize the reasoning so far. According to the Functional Theory of Representation, having the job of being caused by Y suffices for representing Y. A bit more precisely, having the job of being caused by Y suffices for representing one's cause (whatever it might be) as Y, whether or not it is indeed Y. We have just seen that there are things that meet this condition but which are, on their face, not representations: open faucet valves and extended fingers. Hence, having the job of being caused by Y does not suffice for representing (one's actual cause) as Y. A genuine representation purports to portray a thing as being some way or other. When I say "Dinah is in the kitchen," I use Dinah' to refer to a person, portraying her as being in the kitchen. According to the Functional Theory, when X has the job of being caused by Y, X purports to portray its cause (whatever it might be) as Y. But that seems false. Just because X has the job of being caused by Y does not mean that X purports to portray its cause in any way at all. Think of the faucet. Suppose the valve is open not because the knob has been turned but because it has been pried open by a bar. That does not imply that the open valve portrays the prying as a turning of the knob. Indeed, it is implausible that the open valve portrays, refers to, or picks out anything at all.

For these reasons, among others, although the Functional Theory of Representation is alluring, ingenious even, many theorists reject it.[24] So, although most plants satisfy the Theory's conditions for having representations, the Theory itself is questionable, and doesn't give us a strong reason to think plants have representations, or strong information.

7. Memory or Proto-Memory?

While there are a few other theories of representation, none are likely to support the idea that plants have representations, or strong information. These theories tend to have a higher bar, requiring complex cognitive processes, social norms, and even language.[25]

The oscillations shown by roots and shoots certainly can seem to involve representations, since they display a form of error-correction, which can seem to require a representation of the goal. However, as Richard Firn contends, theses oscillations are mere negative feedback loops.[26] A feedback loop is a process that feeds back into itself; that is, it reacts to the effects of its own activity. A *negative* feedback loop is one that diminishes or decreases its activity in response to an increase in an effect of that activity. For instance, a conventional oven involves a negative feedback loop. The heating coil warms, the oven warms, reaching a set temperature, the heating coil ceases warming, the oven cools, the heating element warms again, reaching the set temperature again, and the heating coil ceases warming again, and so on. But feedback loops do not require representations (or strong information).[27] A process that counts as a feedback loop requires only responsiveness to its own effects. And a negative feedback loop is a process that simply has a tendency to diminish its activity (warming the heating coil), given some magnitude of its effects (the temperature in the oven). That's all.

The fact that plants encode, store, and retrieve only weak information can seem to leave us stuck saying that plants don't differ from rocks or puddles, non-living things. Happily, we are no longer stuck with that result. For it is also true that plant parts or organs have the *job* of carrying weak information; that is, the job of their various states is to be caused by various circumstances in their environment. Rocks and other non-living things aren't like that. Having jobs or functions distinguishes living things from non-living things. Unlike rocks, plants are not merely responsive to stimuli, but *purposefully* responsive; when all goes well, their responses serve the plant. And when things don't go well, the plant is in danger. No such thing can be literally said of a mere rock. And—what is deeply intriguing—having jobs or functions *natively*, without bestowal by a designer or a user, distinguishes organisms from artifacts.[28]

These considerations point the way for thinking about whether plants *act*.

Notes

1 (Scott, 2008), (Calvo & Keijzer, 2011), and (Chamowitz, 2013) claim that the Venus flytrap remembers. Chamowitz dedicates a chapter to the topic of plant memory.
2 (Cvrckova, Lipavska, & Zarsky, 2009) and (Calvo & Keijzer, 2011) claim this is a case of memory.
3 (Cvrckova, Lipavska, & Zarsky, 2009) and (Chamowitz, 2013) claim root behavior generally involves a form of memory.
4 (Jaffe, Telewski, & Cooke, 1984), (Trewavas, 2003), and (Chamowitz, 2013) suggest that a form of memory is involved here.
5 See, for instance, (Sternberg, 2008) and (Sutton, 2010).
6 See, for instance, (Sternberg, 2008) and (Sutton, 2010).
7 See, for instance, (Sternberg, 2008) and (Shettleworth, 2009).
8 (Pavlov, 1928). See also (Shettleworth, 2009).
9 See, for instance, (Cho, Heberlein, & Wolf, 2004).
10 (Cvrckova, Lipavska, & Zarsky, 2009) and (Chamowitz, 2013) claim this is a plausible case of memory.
11 (Calvo, 2007).
12 (Trewavas, 2003).
13 (Gagliano, Renton, Depczynski, & Mancuso, 2014).
14 (Shannon & Weaver, 1949). For an overview on information, see (Godfrey-Smith, 2008) and (Adriaans, 2012).

15 The locus classicus for this idea is (Dretske, Explaining Behavior, 1989). (Millikan, 1984) is an important precursor and alternative, tersely summarized in (Millikan, 1989a). For an up-to-date overview of this sort of theory, see (Neander, 2004/2012).
16 For a representative collection, see (Allen, Bekoff, & Lauder, 1998). For an overview of talk of "teleology"—goal-directedness—in biology, see (Allen, 2003).
17 (Cummins, 1975).
18 See, for instance, (Millikan, 1989), which shares much in common with (Wright, 1973).
19 For that type of criticism, see (Cummins, 2002). For a reply, see (Perlman, 2010).
20 See, for instance, (Kitcher, 1993).
21 Again, this is roughly the view of (Dretske, 1989). Another prominent but more complicated theory is that of (Millikan, 1984).
22 Or, more precisely, states of X represent states of Y when states of X were selected for being caused by states of Y.
23 Dretske himself discusses this implication in (Dretske, 1999).
24 See, for instance, (Fodor, 1990).
25 See, for instance, (Davidson, 1975/2001) and (Brandom, 2000).
26 (Firn, 2004).
27 Feedback loops do, of course, involve weak representations, but that is relatively uninteresting for the reasons that we have seen.
28 Kant (Kant, 1790/2000) emphasizes this difference. Many have tried to clarify his claims, including Thompson (Thompson, 2007, Ch. 6).

Works Cited

Adriaans, P. (2012, October 6). *Information*. Retrieved from Stanford Encyclopedia of Philosophy: http://plato.stanford.edu/entries/information/
Allen, C. (2003, May 18). *Teleological Notions in Biology*. Retrieved from Stanford Encyclopedia of Philosophy: http://plato.stanford.edu/entries/teleology-biology/
Allen, C., Bekoff, M., & Lauder, G. (Eds.). (1998). *Nature's Purposes*. Cambridge, MA: MIT Press.
Brandom, R. (2000). *Articulating Reasons*. Cambridge, MA: Harvard University Press.
Calvo, P. (2007). The Quest for Cognition in Plant Biology. *Plant Signaling & Behavior, 2*(4), 208–211.
Calvo, P., & Keijzer, F. (2011). Plants: Adaptive Behavior, Root-Brains, and Minimal Cognition. *Adaptive Behavior, 19*(3), 155–171.
Chamowitz, D. (2013). *What a Plant Knows*. New York: Scientific American.
Cho, W., Heberlein, U., & Wolf, F. (2004). Habituation of an Odorant-Induced Startle Response in Drosophila. *Genes, Brain, and Behavior, 3*(3), 127–137.
Cummins, R. (1975). Functional Analysis. *Journal of Philosophy, 72*(20), 741–765.
Cummins, R. (2002). Neo-Teleology. In A. Ariew, R. E. Cummins, & M. Perlman (Eds.), *Functions: New Essays in the Philosophy of Psychology and Biology*. New York: Oxford University Press.
Cvrckova, F., Lipavska, H., & Zarsky, V. (2009). Plant Intelligence: Why, Why Not or Where? *Plant Signaling & Behavior, 4*(5), 394–399.

Davidson, D. (1975/2001). Thought and Talk. In D. Davidson (Ed.), *Inquiries Into Truth and Interpretation* (2nd ed., pp. 155–170). New York: Oxford University Press.

Dretske, F. (1989). *Explaining Behavior*. Cambridge, MA: MIT Press.

Dretske, F. (1999). Machines, Plants, and Animals. *Erkenntnis, 51*(1), 19–31.

Firn, R. (2004). Plant Intelligence: An Alternative Point of View. *Annals of Botany, 93*(4), 345–351.

Fodor, J. (1990). *A Theory of Content and Other Essays*. Cambridge, MA: MIT Press.

Gagliano, M., Renton, M., Depczynski, M., & Mancuso, S. (2014). Experience Teaches Plants to Learn Faster and Forget Slower. *Oecologia, 175*, 63–72.

Godfrey-Smith, P. (2008). Information in Biology. In D. Hull (Ed.), *Cambridge Companion to Philosophy of Biology* (pp. 103–119). New York: Cambridge University Press.

Jaffe, M., Telewski, F., & Cooke, P. (1984). Thigmomorphogenesis: On the Mechanical Properties of Mechanically Perturbed Bean Plants. *Plant Physiology, 62*, 73–78.

Kant, I. (1790/2000). *Critique of the Power of Judgment* (A. Wood, Ed.). New York: Cambridge University Press.

Kitcher, P. (1993). Function and Design. *Midwest Studies in Philosophy, 18*(1), 379–397.

Millikan, R. (1984). *Language, Thought and Other Biological Categories*. Cambridge, MA: MIT Press.

Millikan, R. (1989a). Biosemantics. *The Journal of Philosophy, 86*(6), 281–297.

Millikan, R. (1989b). In Defense of Proper Functions. *Philosophy of Science, 56*(2), 288–302.

Neander, K. (2004/2012). *Teleological Theories of Mental Content*. Retrieved from Stanford Encyclopedia of Philosophy: http://plato.stanford.edu/entries/content-teleological/

Pavlov, I. (1928). *Lectures on Conditioned Reflexes* (W. Gantt, Trans.). London: Allen and Unwin.

Perlman, M. (2010). Traits Have Evolved to Function the Way They Do Because of a Past Advantage. In F. J. Ayala & R. Arp (Eds.), *Contemporary Debates in the Philosophy of Biology* (pp. 53–71). New York: Blackwell.

Scott, P. (2008). *Physiology and Behavior of Plants*. Hoboken, NJ: Wiley & Sons.

Shannon, C., & Weaver, W. (1949). *The Mathematical Theory of Communication*. Urbana-Champaign, IL: University of Illinois Press.

Shettleworth, S. (2009). *Cognition, Evolution, and Behavior* (2nd ed.). New York: Oxford University Press.

Sternberg, R. (2008). *Cognitive Psychology* (5th ed.). Belmont, CA: Wadsworth.

Sutton, J. (2010, February 3). *Memory*. Retrieved from Stanford Encyclopedia of Philosophy: http://plato.stanford.edu/entries/memory/

Trewavas, A. (2003). Aspects of Plant Intelligence. *Annals of Botany, 92*(1), 1–20.

Wright, L. (1973). Functions. *The Philosophical Review, 82*(2), 139–168.

5 Acting

1. Restless Plants

Caramelized brown sugar and rum, vanilla ice cream, and bananas. Oh, Bananas Foster, how I love thee. I hate waiting for bananas to ripen. A good trick is to store unripe (green) ones in a paper bag with a ripe one. They ripen faster that way. In fact, although it cannot be just any fruit, other ('climacteric') fruits would work too, such as pears, avocadoes, apples, peaches, kiwis, plums, nectarines, or oranges.

Ripeness hastens ripening. (It is a positive feedback loop.) Doing so helps the fruit of a tree to ripen at the same time. Different parts of trees, especially large trees, experience different conditions over the course of the day: there are microclimates. Some parts get more sunlight than others; some get lower temperatures than others; some encounter stronger breezes than others. Those conditions affect rates of growth. Since ripeness hastens ripening, there is a better chance that all fruits ripen at approximately the same time. Among other things, since fruits are tasty vehicles for seeds, that increases the chances that seeds will be available at the same time. That can be good for the propagation of the species if there is a specific time of year when there is a greater chance that fruit is likely to be foraged, ingested, and carried off in the stomachs of various creatures.[1]

As Daniel Chamowitz reports in *What a Plant Knows*, for a very long time, at some level, people have known that ripeness hastens ripening. Ancient Egyptians, for instance, stored unripe figs with ripe figs, cutting the ripe figs open. A natural hunch about how this works is that ripe fruit 'gives off' something that affects other fruit. Nearly five millennia later, in the middle of the nineteenth century, with the advent of gas lighting, there were reports that plants around street lamps were growing strangely gnarled, often over-growing.[2] In 1901, Dimitry Neljubow showed that ethylene was the substance causing such growth. Pea plants that he exposed to it grew short, thick, and curled; unexposed plants grew relatively tall, skinny, and straight.

Wild lima beans do something more impressive (Figure 5.1). They are intermittently attacked by one type of mite, a small arthropod, *T. urticae* (Figure 5.2). In response, the plant releases various compounds, including methyl salicylate, which attracts a second type of mite, *P. persimilis*, which attacks the first type of mite, effectively defending the bean plants. In addition, neighboring bean plants that have not been attacked also begin to produce methyl salicylate, seemingly in anticipation of an attack by mites.[3]

Acacia trees do something similar. On a game ranch in South Africa, Wouter Van Hoven was investigating the sudden death of 3,000 kudu (a type of antelope). Although kudu do not normally graze on acacia trees, on the overcrowded ranch, he found that they are forced to do so. But when the

Figure 5.1 Wild lima bean (*Phaseolus lunatus*)

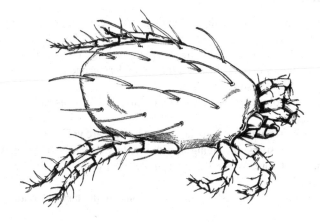

Figure 5.2 Mite (*Tetranychus urticae*)

acacia trees are persistently grazed on, they release tannins, which the kudu ingest, which impedes their digestion, and they die. Moreover, like the lima bean, neighboring acacia that have not been grazed on also start to produce tannins. It seems to be a pre-emptive defense.[4]

Chemomorphism, physiological changes in response to chemicals, makes it tempting to say that plants communicate with each other. As if the banana calls out: "Now is the time to ripen." Or the acacia warns its neighbor: "Release the tannins!"

In Dov Keller's phrase, plants certainly are restless.[5] But they do not just bend in the breeze, or passively undergo changes in size, location, and orientation. Rather, they make things happen, on their own. Furthermore, as we saw in the previous chapter, a lot of what they do is not merely haphazard, but instead has a point, helping the plant thrive and reproduce. Thus, plants appear to initiate things on their own, and for their own good. That can tempt us to say that they are not just active, but that they *act*—voluntarily, intentionally, or on purpose.

Do they?

At this point, I wouldn't be surprised if you doubted it. If plants don't really perceive, feel, or remember, then it seems unlikely that they act in any way that requires a mind. Perception, feeling, and memory might be necessary for having a mind at all. Or perception, feeling, and memory might be necessary for mind-involving action.

Those reasons are compelling, but not decisive. In this chapter, we will unearth a key claim underlying them: minds require representations. One might reject that claim.

Let us look more closely at voluntary action.

2. Voluntary Action

Breathing, sleeping, dreaming, sweating, waking, walking, flipping a light switch, brewing tea, sitting upright, sipping tea, holding a book, reading, salivating, digesting tea, blinking, burping, writing, talking, planning dinner, stretching, yawning, tiring, aging, wondering about my son's future, playing ice hockey, smiling.

Which are voluntary? Which are involuntary? Take a moment before seeing my answer.

I say: walking, writing, and playing ice hockey are voluntary; by contrast, salivating, digesting, and aging are involuntary. What about stretching or yawning? Not sure. While I don't usually elect or plan to do them, I can control them.

What exactly distinguishes voluntary from involuntary behavior?

One good idea: your voluntary acts are ones you genuinely perform; involuntary acts are ones that simply happen with you or your body. Perhaps with that idea in mind, in his celebrated *Philosophical Investigations*, posthumously published in 1953, Ludwig Wittgenstein asks: "What is left over if I subtract the fact that my arm goes up from the fact that I raise my arm?"[6] What makes a movement of my body count as an action of mine, something *I* do, rather than something that merely goes on with my body?

For early experimental psychologists, from roughly 1860 to 1900 in England, Europe, and America, the essential difference between voluntary and 'reflex' action was the involvement of 'ideas' or 'consciousness,' a mind. Reflex actions required no learning; a creature just does them; they just happen. A cat tenses when startled, or blinks when a bird zooms toward its face. By contrast, non-reflex or voluntary actions were learned, reflecting previous experiences. After some time in one of Edward Thorndike's puzzle boxes, cats became increasingly efficient at getting out. Reflex actions were fixed and inflexible. A creature tends not to have control over them; given the right stimulus, they just happen. Startling and blinking just happen. Non-reflex actions, by contrast, could be learned and forgotten; they could be controlled, for they are not invariably produced in the presence of a given stimulus. If a cat is satiated, it will take longer getting out of Thorndike's puzzle box, for it isn't motivated to try. Because voluntary actions depend on experience, learning, and memory, and can be controlled, they were thought to require a mind. Reflex actions did not require a mind, because they did not depend on experience, learning, or memory, and generally cannot be controlled.

What about, say, Pavlov's dogs, who reflexively salivated upon seeing food? After several occasions on which the food was immediately preceded by a bell, they salivated simply when they heard the bell alone. That salivating 'just happened.' The dogs didn't have any interesting form of control over it. True, if they weren't hungry and heard the bell, they did not salivate or salivated less. So, they didn't *always* salivate upon hearing the bell. But that doesn't imply that they can control whether they salivate. The tendency to salivate in response to the bell seems like a reflex, but clearly it was the result of prior experience and learning. Which is it: reflex or non-reflex?

Watson's Behaviorism was an especially adamant rejection of the distinction between reflex and learned-hence-mind-involving action. Holding that the mind was nothing but tendencies or dispositions to behave in various ways, he contended that no behaviors, no matter how sophisticated or learned, involved a mind. All behaviors were instead just elaborate "reflexes," or responses to stimuli. With his studies of "operant conditioning" in rats and pigeons, B.F. Skinner carried that way of thinking further. In a simple version of these studies, a rat sits in a small box with a lever, which if pressed will release a food pellet. That food pellet "reinforces" the act of pressing the lever, encouraging the rat to do it again. According to Skinner, the rat simply developed a disposition to press the lever, and required no additional mind or memory.

Although Radical Behaviorism was influential, especially in America, it was only one sort of reaction to questions about the line between reflex and non-reflex behavior. Others, including Pavlov himself, thought that many reflex or reflex-like behaviors required a mind. His dogs learn and so remember to salivate upon hearing the bell, and they can forget or un-learn that reaction. Why do the dogs *salivate* when they hear the bell—why does a bell provoke a response appropriate for *food*? A plausible conjecture is that the bell makes the dogs think of food, perhaps calling to mind its image or scent, a *representation*.

Other studies, done a bit later, also pointed towards representations. In his groundbreaking book, *Aus dem Leben der Bienen* (*The Dancing Bees*), published in 1927, Karl von Frisch explained how honeybees use "dances" to tell their fellow bees where to find food. Foragers return to the hive and move about on the wall of the hive as others look on. Their movements correlate systematically with the distance and direction of the food source they have recently visited.[7] In turn, onlookers systematically arrive at that very location. The dances seem to be a sort of language.[8]

In 1948, in "Cognitive Maps in Rats and Men," on the basis of two decades of research, Edward Tolman argued that rats construct "cognitive maps" of mazes that they have traveled. After just a few opportunities to explore a maze, positively reinforced by food, rats develop a disposition to take the correct path on subsequent occasions. You might think that they simply learn that specific path, a sequence of turns. However, Tolman provided compelling evidence that they have something like an inner map of the layout of the maze, a representation of the spatial relations of the parts. Roughly a third of his rats preferentially took shortcuts that they had never before traveled. These rats were able to "figure out" that some path that they had never taken would get them to the end, and faster[9] (Figure 5.3).

Von Frisch's and Tolman's work encouraged the idea that nonhuman animals have ideas, hence minds, thus challenging the Cartesian belief that only humans have minds. It pressed the question of which behaviors exactly require a mind, blurring the line between those that do, and those that don't. It also encouraged the idea that nonhuman animals can produce, even embody, representations.

As I mentioned back in the first chapter, in the 1950s, a substantive and powerful alternative to behaviorism instigated the Cognitive Revolution in psychology: the Computational Theory of Mind. The core idea was that a

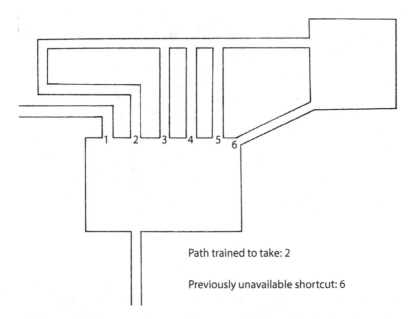

Path trained to take: 2

Previously unavailable shortcut: 6

Figure 5.3 Edward Tolman's rat maze

mind is like—or, more provocatively, *just is*—a computer. Very roughly: a mind receives input, performs computations (calculations, or inferences) on that input, and produces an output. That idea has become so familiar that it can seem uninteresting, but in fact it was novel and deeply interesting. Its interest and novelty stems from a fairly rigorous characterization of the notion of a *computer*, which grew out of the work of Alan Turing.[10]

A computer is a formal system. A formal system is like a game that specifies a set of pieces or tokens, a starting position, and a set of legal moves. Think of the peg game you can find at roadside restaurants, such as *Cracker Barrel* (Figure 5.4). There are fifteen holes, arrayed in an equilateral triangle, and fourteen pegs. The game starts with a peg in every hole but one. A peg may be validly moved to an empty hole only if there is a single peg between that peg and the hole. That is, a peg can reach an empty hole only by 'jumping' an adjacent peg. When a peg is 'jumped,' it must be removed from its hole, which is left empty. The game is over when no valid moves remain. The peg game exemplifies other notable features of formal systems. They are definite: it is never ambiguous whether a position or move is valid. They are also finitely checkable: whether a position or move is valid can be checked in a finite number of steps.

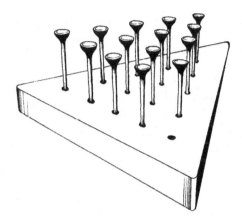

Figure 5.4 Peg solitaire

An *automatic* formal system makes valid moves on its own. Imagine an automated peg board game. In addition to the pegs and board, there would be a mechanism for inserting and removing pegs, one which placed pegs in a starting position, and which moved them according to the rules.[11] Since, at any given point in a game, often more than one valid move is available, there would also be a move chooser, which would also need to be automated.

A computer is an *interpreted* automatic formal system: its tokens, positions, and moves stand for, mean, or represent something. You could play the peg game without an actual board or pegs, using just a piece of paper and a pencil, with X's for holes-with-pegs and O's for empty holes. Indeed, the game could even be 'played' (or expressed) as a series of strings of characters. The first string would express the starting position. Subsequent strings would specify which holes are empty or filled after each move in the game. What matters is that the game starts and proceeds in accord with the rules; the starting position and all intervening positions must be valid (legal, or permissible). Suitably automated, this version of the game would be an interpreted automatic formal system, for the strings of characters are *symbols*, items that *stand for* or *represent* positions of pegs on the board. A calculator is a more familiar example of an interpreted automatic formal system. The states that appear on its screen stand for numbers. More generally, a computer is an automatic formal system whose states (or 'positions') have an interpretation, a systematic specification of what they stand for, mean, or represent.

According to the Computational Theory of Mind, a mind is a "semantic engine," a machine that systematically manipulates representations (meaningful items) in accord with rules.[12] To highlight the importance of representations—to which I will return shortly—it is sometimes called the "Computational-Representational Theory of Mind."[13] According to the theory, behavior involves a mind when it involves computations, rule-governed manipulation of representations. What's left over when I subtract the fact that my arm goes up from the fact that I raised my arm? A representation, says the Computational Theory—a representation of moving my arm.[14]

Cognitive science grew out of the Computational Theory of Mind, as exemplified in Miller, Galanter, and Pribram's *Plans and the Structure of Behavior* of 1960, and later Jerry Fodor's *The Language of Thought* of 1975, and the "physical symbol system hypothesis" articulated by Allen Newell and Herbert Simon in 1976.[15] Many (if not most) contemporary cognitive scientists espouse a descendent of it. They take for granted the idea that a mind is a computer: a device that systematically manipulates representations; they explain behavior by explaining how it involves a systematic manipulation of representations.

3. Plant Action

If the Computational Theory of Mind is correct, then plants act voluntarily or 'on purpose' only if they act in ways that involve representations. And we have already found that while plants have *weak* information, there is no good reason to think they have *strong* information, genuine representations. We have found no good reason to think that gravitropism, phototropism, photoperiodism, or thigmotropism involve inner states or occurrences that *portray* something in some way or other, and can thus be accurate or inaccurate. So, if the Computational Theory of Mind is correct, it is doubtful that plants act in ways that require a mind.

Some cognitive scientists are not careful about the difference between weak and strong information, or about what qualifies as a genuine representation.[16] When they mention representations or representational states, they do not take care to say whether they are talking about things that portray something in some way or other, and can thus be accurate or inaccurate. In many cases, it seems as though 'representation' could be replaced by 'intermediary'; or 'representation of X' could be replaced by 'effect of X.'

Other cognitive scientists—and most philosophers of cognitive science— are sensitive to the difference, stressing that the Computational Theory requires genuine representations, not just weak information.[17] It is precisely the representational character of the states that computations are performed on that explains why certain behaviors are performed.[18] For instance, it is because the inner state of Tolman's rats is *of* the maze, its shape and layout, that the rats manage to take a shortcut. Similarly, it is because Pavlov's dogs are in a state that *represents* food when they hear the bell that those dogs attempt to move toward where they expect food to be. This would also explain why, when the dogs are satiated and hear the bell, they do not attempt to move in that direction.

So, if the Computational Theory is right, then plant behaviors don't involve a mind, since they don't involve representations.

Even chemomorphisms—those apparently 'communicative' behaviors—don't require representations or strong information. The signals themselves cannot be genuinely false or inaccurate. Instead, we can grant that a sent or received signal might not perform its proper function. For instance, on the sender side, the release of ethylene by a banana might fail to stimulate other bananas to ripen—there might be none nearby, or there might be a very strong wind. On the receiver side, ripening in response to ethylene might occur even when it's not the right time of the season or year, as when botanists spray bananas with ethylene. These signals simply malfunction. We need not say they are false or inaccurate, a mis-portrayal of things. Furthermore, a plant that sends a chemical signal need not have a representation of what it is reacting to—what its signal is a signal *of*—or of what the result of sending the signal might be. Likewise, a plant that receives a chemical signal need not have a representation of the state of the plant that sent it, or of anything at all.

This is a big lesson: the whole case against plant minds hangs on the claim that they don't have representations. That is the main reason for thinking they don't perceive, feel, or remember, or act voluntarily or 'on purpose.' In a tidy argument:

1   Having a mind requires having representations.
2   But plants don't have representations.
3   *Therefore*, plants don't have minds.

That should be surprising. It is hardly obvious that representations are required for having a mind. Before you opened this book, suppose someone had said to you, "No way plants have minds; they don't have representations." You might have scoffed: "Why should that matter? What do representations have to do with it?"

However, the idea that the mind is a collection of representations has deep historical roots. You can find it already in Plato and Aristotle. It is recurrently alluring.

When I write, I often think about my friend Mark, what I'd say to him, and what he'd ask me. We went to graduate school together. Through many conversations about many things, I came to depend on, trust, and value his judgment. He now has four young kids and a job, so I can't expect him to read everything I write, nor even every polished thing I write. Instead, I imagine talking with him. Sometimes I see him on the old couch in his old apartment. Imagining Mark helps me write better.

A genuine marvel, that capacity we have to think about people who aren't here with us, about what they used to say or do, and about what they might say or do, even though they haven't said or done it. We are not always correct or accurate, but even that is impressive: We can think about things otherwise than how they actually are, even if by mistake.

That suggests that representations, *re*-presentations or recurrences of something that was once present, are the coin of the mental realm.

If so, it is doubtful that plants have minds.

However, there is one last influential idea about representations that offers some hope for thinking plants have them. Daniel Dennett has provocatively proposed that a thing (a system, a creature) counts as having representations simply if it is explanatorily useful to think of that thing as having them; there is no more (or less) to it than that.[19] For instance, since it is useful to think of a rat as having a representation when explaining its journey through a maze, that rat has a representation. Thus, Dennett is commonly seen as proposing a sort of instrumentalism about representations; they exist to the extent that they are explanatorily useful posits.

Dennett holds that to think of a thing as having representations is to take a "stance" towards it, an interpretive-explanatory attitude or strategy. Call it the Representation Stance.[20] He contrasts this stance with two others. Thinking of a thing as a physical system—subject, say, to Newton's three laws—is to take the "Physical Stance" towards that system. This stance does not require positing representations. The third stance is the "design stance," one in which we treat a thing as being designed by an intelligent designer. Dennett illustrates how the three different stances can be fruitfully taken towards one and the same object: a chess game on a computer, such as an app on a phone. In playing against the computer, you will treat it as trying to win, as trying to come up with the best, most sensible move at each stage. You treat it as having beliefs, desires, and intentions, hence representations. In this stance, you don't particularly care that it was designed by a team of programmers, or made of plastic and metal. However, suppose that certain legal moves aren't permitted. A programmer might be called, asked to find where the program is going wrong, where the design went awry or was wrongly implemented. The programmer won't need to think of the computer as having any representations at all; it is irrelevant to his or her purposes. (He or she will, however, think of the programmers as having representations, plans for how the program should behave.) And if the computer consistently shuts off at a certain point in play, an electrical engineer might be brought in, treating the computer (or phone) simply as a physical system. The fact that it was designed and is supposed to store a program does not matter. What matters for the engineer is how electricity moves through the device—perhaps it overheats after certain periods of time.

Now take the Representation Stance toward a plant, a case of gravitropism. Why do the roots grow this way? Because the statoliths represent that way as down, and roots aim for or want to go down.

If we accept Dennett's instrumentalist suggestion, this plant counts as having a representation *if* treating it as having a representation has been explanatorily useful.

Has it been? It can seem so. Roots grow as they do because the statoliths represent where down lies. But that use of representation is dubious. It doesn't make root growth easier to understand. We are left wondering, for instance, how the statoliths manage to represent where down is, or anything at all. We are also left wondering how this information is 'communicated' to and 'interpreted' by the rest of the plant. Talk of representation starts to seem like metaphor or shorthand for something else. Furthermore, invoking a representation seems gratuitous. It does not allow us to understand something that we could not otherwise understand. We could instead say that the root grows *this way* because the statoliths move in *that direction* which stimulates the production of auxin, and its transmission to the opposite side of the root, causing cells there to expand more. And these arrangements are in place because of a very long evolutionary history.

So, while Dennett's suggestion might seem appealing, it does not provide especially compelling grounds for thinking that plants have representations.

Even if a lack of representations implies that plants don't act voluntarily or 'on purpose,' we have a way to appreciate why they seem to do so, for we know that many of their behaviors have functions or jobs. Many plant parts and their processes are *adaptations*, traits that have been 'selected for.' Although each might initially have been the result of a random mutation in a lone plant, the advantage that each conferred on that lone plant allowed the trait to be inherited by thousands of subsequent generations. Just as plant parts and behaviors do not need a designer, so too can they be purposive without being voluntary or done on purpose.

4. The Root Assumption

In this chapter, our specific goal was to consider whether plants act, voluntarily. The Computational-Representational Theory of Mind holds that doing so requires representations. Since we don't have good reason to think that plants have representations, the Theory implies that plants don't act voluntarily.

The big lesson of this chapter is that the best case against plant minds—which has accumulated across the preceding chapters—depends on the claim that minds require representations. To perceive, feel, remember, and act (voluntarily) requires the capacity to form representations. Thus excavated, this root claim can be scrutinized, and potentially rejected. Indeed, some astute cognitive scientists and philosophers deny that representations are necessary for having a mind.

In the next and final chapter, I will pursue that possibility, arguing that plants do have minds.

Notes

1 See, for instance, (Bidlack & Jansky, 2010) and (Mauseth, 2008).
2 See, for instance, (Saltveit, Yang, & Kim, 1997).
3 (De Boer & Dicke, 2004).
4 This story was originally reported in (Hughes, 1990), and subsequently covered in many other places, including the documentary film *In the Mind of Plants* (Mitsch, 2013).
5 (Keller, 2011).
6 (Wittgenstein, 1953/1958, p. 161 (§621)).
7 The best supporting data are reported in (Riley, Greggers, Smith, Reynolds, & Menzel, 2005).
8 Von Frisch developed these ideas further in (von Frisch, 1967/1993).
9 Tolman's work, along with other challenges to behaviorism, is nicely summarized in (Rey, 1997). See also (Shettleworth, 2009).
10 I am relying on the presentation of computers in (Haugeland, 1985).
11 How many starting positions are there? There are fifteen different holes, any of which could be the one left empty at the start. But some of these holes are effectively equivalent to others. For instance, the holes at the vertices are equivalent to each other. Rotating the board shows this. So, in fact, there are only five *unique* starting positions.
12 The phrase "semantic engines" comes from (Dennett, 1981).
13 See, for instance, (Rey, 1997).
14 For an overview of cognitive scientific research on voluntary action, see (Hommel, 2003) and (Morsella, 2008). For an influential contemporary philosopher endorsing the same basic idea, see (Dretske, 1989).
15 (Newell & Simon, 1976).
16 See, for instance, (Sternberg, 2008).
17 See, for instance, (Horst, 2009) and (Milkowski, 2013).
18 This point is stressed by (Fodor, 1987) and (Dretske, 1989).
19 See, for instance, (Dennett, 1981).
20 Dennett calls it the "Intentional Stance." Here he is using the word 'intentional' in a way that is probably foreign to most non-philosophers. Here, 'intentional' does *not* mean 'on purpose' or something similar. Instead, in this way of using the word, drawing on a long tradition in philosophy, a thing has intentionality

when it is *about* or *directed at* something else. Thoughts and claims have intentionality, for they are *about* something else. Such things are intentional states or episodes. "Intentional System" is Dennett's phrase for things that have or undergo intentional states or episodes. See, for instance, (Jacob, 2014).

Works Cited

Bidlack, J., & Jansky, S. (2010). *Stern's Introductory Plant Biology* (12th ed.). New York: McGraw-Hill.

De Boer, J., & Dicke, M. (2004). The Role of Methyl Salicylate in Prey Searching Behavior of the Predatory Mite Phytoseiulus Persimilis. *Journal of Chemical Ecology, 30*(2), 255–271.

Dennett, D. (1981). Three Kinds of Intentional Psychology. In D. Dennett (Ed.), *Brainstorms* (pp. 37–61). Cambridge, MA: MIT Press.

Dretske, F. (1989). *Explaining Behavior.* Cambridge, MA: MIT Press.

Fodor, J. (1987). *Psychosemantics.* Cambridge, MA: MIT Press.

Haugeland, J. (1985). *Artificial Intelligence: The Very Idea.* Cambridge, MA: MIT Press.

Hommel, B. (2003). Acquisition and Control of Voluntary Action. In S. Maasen, W. Prinz, & G. Roth (Eds.), *Voluntary Action.* New York: Oxford University Press.

Horst, S. (2009, December 10). *The Computational Theory of Mind.* Retrieved from Stanford Encyclopedia of Mind: http://plato.stanford.edu/entries/computational-mind/

Hughes, S. (1990). Antelope Activate the Acacia's Alarm System. *New Scientist* (1736).

Jacob, P. (2014, October 15). *Intentionality.* Retrieved from Stanford Encyclopedia of Philosophy: http://plato.stanford.edu/entries/intentionality/

Keller, D. (2011). *The Restless Plant.* Cambridge, MA: Cambridge University Press.

Mauseth, J. (2008). *Botany* (4th ed.). Mississauga, ON: Jones & Bartlett.

Milkowski, M. (2013). *The Computational Theory of Mind.* Retrieved from Internet Encyclopedia of Philosophy: www.iep.utm.edu/compmind/

Mitsch, J. (Director). (2013). *In the Mind of Plants* [Motion Picture].

Morsella, E. (2008). The Mechanism of Human Action. In E. Morsella, J. Bargh, & P. Gollwitzer (Eds.), *The Oxford Handbook of Human Action* (pp. 1–34). New York: Oxford University Press.

Newell, A., & Simon, H. (1976). Computer Science as Empirical Inquiry: Symbols and Search. *Communications of the ACM, 19*(3), 113–126.

Rey, G. (1997). *Contemporary Philosophy of Mind.* New York: Blackwell.

Riley, J., Greggers, U., Smith, A., Reynolds, D., & Menzel, R. (2005). The Flight Paths of Honeybees Recruited by the Waggle Dance. *Nature, 435,* 205–207.

Saltveit, M., Yang, S., & Kim, W. (1997). History of the Discovery of Ethylene as a Plant Growth Substance. In S-D. Kung & S-F. Yang (Eds.), *Discoveries in Plant Biology* (Vol. 1, pp. 47–70). River Edge, NJ: World Scientific Publishing.

Shettleworth, S. (2009). *Cognition, Evolution, and Behavior* (2nd ed.). New York: Oxford University Press.

Sternberg, R. (2008). *Cognitive Psychology* (5th ed.). Belmont, CA: Wadsworth.
von Frisch, K. (1967/1993). *The Dance Language and Orientation of Bees* (L. Chadwick, Trans.). Cambridge, MA: Harvard University Press.
Wittgenstein, L. (1953/1958). *Philosophical Investigations* (3rd ed., G. Anscombe, Trans.). New York: Blackwell.

6 Mind in Life

1. Do Plants Have Minds?

Plants grow and bend towards light. Their roots grow into the ground, while their shoots grow up, out of the soil. When roots and shoots are mechanically impeded, they change course. In windy conditions, many will develop thicker stems and branches. When threatened by toxins, many emit signals which are received by neighbors, which help them resist damage. These are some of the many ways in which plants take care of themselves through changing circumstances.

We have considered whether plants perceive, feel, remember, and act. And we have seen that these terms are ambiguous, admitting of stronger and weaker interpretations. On the stronger interpretations, which require plants to have genuine representations (and not merely weak information), plants do not do these things. Thus, there is a compelling argument for thinking that plants do not have minds.

Still, although plants do not have representations, perhaps they do not need representations to have minds. One might think they have minds because, putting it roughly, they take care of themselves. For this suggestion to be compelling, however, we need to get much clearer about it.

That is my aim in this chapter.

2. Minds Without Representations

Consider first: Do minds require representations?

Think about hammering a nail. In my left hand, between my thumb and forefinger, I hold the nail, tip to the wood. In my right, the hammer. Centering the hammer head on the nail head, I tap the nail to sink it. I strike again, getting a sense for the stiffness of the wood. I strike again, adjusting the hammer, my fingers, hand, wrist, and arm, and the force with which I strike. A third time I strike, and the nail head is flush with the wood's surface.

Although I do all of these things when I hammer, I do not consciously think about doing them. When I was learning how to hammer, I probably did. But though I'm no carpenter, I now know how to hammer. I just do it, without thinking, consciously or even unconsciously. For instance, if in the midst of hammering you asked me the approximate degree to which I must cock my wrist on the second strike, I might not be able to tell you or even show you, except by just hitting the nail. When I strike, I just cock my wrist to the proper angle.

Similar things are true of brushing my teeth, buttoning a shirt, unlocking a door, riding a bike, and a great many other activities in which I daily engage. We do a lot of sophisticated stuff without consciously or unconsciously thinking about doing so.

Despite the lack of conscious or unconscious thinking, these activities are recognizably intelligent. They have goals and standards of proper performance to which our movements are sensitive. For instance, the goal of hammering a nail is (commonly, anyway) to make the nail flush with the surface into which one is hammering it. My movements with the hammer and nail are sensitive to that goal; they respond in ways that efficiently bring it about. My adjustments are (often enough) proper, more proper than others, such as trying to strike with the handle, or prematurely giving up.

In the early twentieth century, in opposition to common and arguably dominant conceptions of the human mind and intelligence, a few philosophers, such as Martin Heidegger and John Dewey, made this sort of case.[1] Very roughly, they both opposed the view that any and all genuinely intelligent activity was initiated and sustained by "ideas," which were necessarily "conscious," or reflectively accessible to the actor; intelligent activity required having an idea of one's goal, which guided one's performance. To philosophers like Heidegger and Dewey, such a conception of intelligent activity was excessively "intellectual," making it require "intellect," a capacity for reasoned calculation, as if mundane hammering was akin to encountering an unusual math problem for the first time. They argued that this is clearly not true of lived human experiences. Thinking about hammering while hammering can actually get in the way of hammering properly. Furthermore, lived human experience aside, this intellectualist conception of intelligent activity is also not compelling as an explanatory hypothesis about what goes on in such activity. Specifically, it is not clear that ideas really are necessary to account for the intelligence of all of our intelligent activities. On the "intellectualist" view, the intelligent part of intelligent activity consists strictly in the existence of an idea that precedes the related bodily movements. Those movements themselves are intelligent only because they happen to result from ideas, the fount of intelligence. For Heidegger and Dewey, by contrast, the intelligence of at least some activities lies more in the flexible responsiveness of our bodies. Bodily movements themselves, and even pieces of equipment, workshops, and social arrangements, not just ideas, can be intelligent.

In response to the Cognitive Revolution in psychology, and specifically work in early artificial intelligence, philosophers such as Hubert Dreyfus and John Haugeland wielded a version of this point against the Computational Theory of Mind, which was seen as resembling the older, "intellectualist" conception of intelligent activity.[2] They alleged that not all intelligent activity requires representation and computation.[3]

Their allegation was vindicated by some work in artificial intelligence and robotics. For instance, based on the work of Rodney Brooks at MIT, roboticists designed a robot, named Herbert, to collect empty soda cans around their lab. One way to design such a robot would be to provide it with a complete map of the lab. But there is a way to do it without such a map. One could program it with a set of relatively simple behavioral rules that specify what to do under various conditions. For instance: move forward until impeded; scan for cans; if a can is detected, collect it and move right; if no can is detected, move right; if you cannot move right, rotate ninety degrees and move right. In this way, without a map, Herbert can navigate the perimeter of the lab, collecting cans.

"Anti-intellectualists," like Heidegger, Dewey, Dreyfus, and Haugeland, face a tough question: How can something be directed toward a goal if it doesn't have an "idea" or representation of that goal?

In a 1995 essay, Tim van Gelder, Haugeland's student, pointed to James Watt's centrifugal governor as a paradigm of goal-directed activity without goal-representation[4] (Figure 6.1). This governor 'governs' the speed of a steam engine, aiming to keep it constant. It does so by regulating the amount of steam flowing into the engine through a pipe. As the engine speeds up, the governor proportionally closes the valve on the pipe, reducing the flow of steam into the engine, thus slowing the engine. As the engine slows down, the governor proportionally opens the valve on the pipe, increasing the flow of steam, thus accelerating the engine. One of van Gelder's main points was that Watt's governor governs speed successfully without ever representing current or desired speed (or flow of steam).[5]

3. Plants Have Minds

Enactivism, which I introduced in Chapter Three, also rejects the claim that minds require representations. It maintains that to have a mind is not necessarily to harbor representations—pictures, words, models, maps—of a world outside oneself, but is to disclose (bring forth or 'enact') a world of things that have significance (meaning or value).

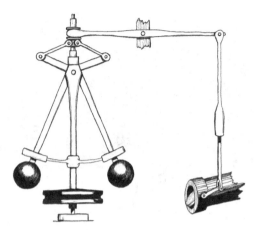

Figure 6.1 James Watt's centrifugal governor

Thus, we have some resources for rejecting the Computational Theory of Mind, and its attendant claim that mind requires representation, hence the case against plant minds.

Since plants are autopoietic-and-adaptive ("autopoietic" in Thompson's more generous sense), Enactivism also provides support for thinking that plants have minds—or, if you want to be cautious, proto-minds or minimal minds. Recall that Enactivism holds that to have a mind is to 'enact' or disclose a value-laden world, an environment or niche, an array of things that matter in various ways. It contends further that all living things do just that; through their activities, they bring forth or disclose an array of things that matter in various ways. They manage to do that because they are autopoietic and adaptive. Autopoietic: self-producing. Adaptive: adjusting effectively in response to conditions that affect viability. Being autopoietic-and-adaptive discloses a value-laden world, a milieu or niche. This is not a value-neutral space, but a field of things that have significance, opportunities, and threats, things that help and hinder the continuation of the self.

Linger a while over how thoroughly autopoietic (in Thompson's broad sense) plants are. Step with me into the glade of the mind. See the teacup magnolia over yonder, lit by the late afternoon spring sun? A beautiful sight, but it is deceptively easy to think that the tree just sits there, as if it were always there, looking lovely (Figure 6.2).

How did it get there? Decades ago, a seed settled, pressed unwittingly into the soil by squirrels, raccoons, chipmunks, and deer. It arrived along a network of impromptu streamlets, the result of spring rains, from another

Figure 6.2 Teacup magnolia (*Magnolia* × *soulangeana*)

teacup magnolia. On that tree, on the stigma of one of its flowers, there had landed a grain of pollen, borne on the wind from yet another teacup magnolia. It extended a tube downward into the ovary of the flower, fertilizing the ovum that waited there (Figure 6.3). The resulting seed was a marvelous thing: the tiny germ of what would become an enormous tree, shrouded in a case of nutrients, shrouded again in a hard, protective coat, able to withstand substantial temperature changes and mechanical perturbations until it came to rest, here in our glade.

A lot had to happen for its shoot to make its way to the surface. Absorbing water from the surrounding soil, its cells expanded and then divided, over and again, creating nuclei, ribosomes, endoplasmic reticula, mitochondria, vacuoles, chloroplasts, and plasma membranes. Surrounding the membranes were rigid walls made of cellulose, a type of carbohydrate, the main substance in wood. They also contained various lipids, which are waterproof. Cells eventually differentiated and specialized, forming distinct types of tissue, such as the epidermis. Walls of the cells of the epidermis created cutin and other waxes that are indigestible and unappealing to many bacteria, fungi, and animals. In addition to creating epidermal cells with waxy walls, some plants, such as acacia, produce special chemicals that lure defenders or repel attackers. Wild tobacco (*Nicotiana attenuata*) is an interesting example (Figure 6.4). When it is attacked by various insects, it produces nicotine, which is poisonous to most insects. However, the nicotine doesn't affect hornworm caterpillars (Figure 6.5). When grazed upon

Figure 6.3 Parts of a pistil: stigma, stile, ovary

Figure 6.4 Wild tobacco (*Nicotiana attenuata*)

by these caterpillars, wild tobacco releases a variety of chemicals ('green leaf volatiles'), which attract big-eyed bugs, which eat the eggs and larvae of the caterpillars, defending the tobacco plant.[6] Returning to our fledgling magnolia, it could not have told us what it was doing, nor did it envision the end result, but still it did them, with impressive efficiency and effectiveness.

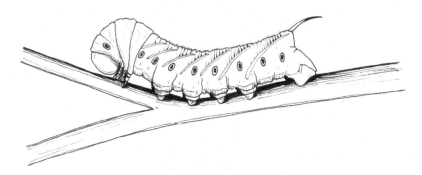

Figure 6.5 Hornworm caterpillar (*Manduca sexta*)

Once it broke ground, to get energy through photosynthesis, our magnolia seedling needed light and carbon dioxide for photosynthesis. First building buds along its stem, it created branches and leaves, which increased its access to light and carbon dioxide.

Leaves helped the young tree create energy, but they were also a burden, for they increased the mechanical stress on the whole plant, since they caught wind, acting like sails. Thus, the plant created cells that were not so rigid that branches or the stem would crack under temporary but sustained and substantial increases of pressure. Exposure to wind, like exposure to sunlight, depends on atmospheric conditions, topography, and the size and distribution of neighboring plants. None of these is fixed, but instead varies over time. To survive, our young tree had to adjust.

Below the surface, in the soil, the roots continued to grow, increasing the surface area that was exposed to water, increasing how much water and nutrients the plant absorbed. The larger root system also helped anchor the plant, counterbalancing the increase in size above the surface. Without a good anchor, the plant would have tipped over, not only reducing access to light, but potentially cracking the trunk, the plant's central vascular system, exposing it to pests and diseases. As the trunk and branches grew, so too must the roots have grown.

Photosynthesis is the main means by which our magnolia, like all plants, created energy, converting water and carbon dioxide, in the presence of sunlight, into glucose, with oxygen as a byproduct. In fact, photosynthesis, which occurs also in some bacteria, is the primary means by which any energy whatsoever becomes available to all organisms. Autotrophs are organisms that create their own energy, primarily through photosynthesis. Heterotrophs are organisms that do not create their own energy, but instead get it from other organisms. Some heterotrophs get their energy from only other heterotrophs. For instance, lions are carnivores. But that cannot be true of all heterotrophs. Some must get their energy from autotrophs. Otherwise, there would be an impossible chain of heterotrophs getting energy from heterotrophs, without energy ever initially entering the chain. Without autotrophs, there would be no energy for heterotrophs to consume. Photosynthesis is thus essential for every living thing.

Although it was necessary for our magnolia to survive, photosynthesis is risky. It requires both carbon dioxide and water, but in getting carbon dioxide, plants wind up losing water. Gas exchange is the process by which a plant absorbs carbon dioxide and releases oxygen. It occurs through hundreds of stomata, pores found mainly on the underside of leaves (Figure 6.6). They are spaces bordered by two 'guard cells.' When those cells swell with water, the stoma opens. When they are not swollen, the stoma is closed (Figure 6.7). Typically, stomata open during the day, when sunlight is available for photosynthesis. They close at night, when sunlight isn't available

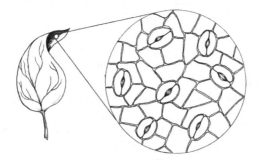

Figure 6.6 Stomata

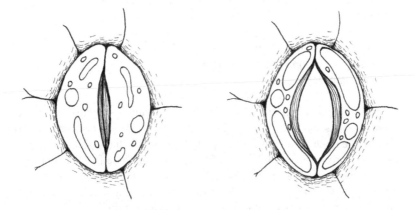

Figure 6.7 Open and closed stoma

for photosynthesis. Gas exchange inevitably results in water loss, or transpiration, because water vapor escapes through the stomata. So, our magnolia must have carefully regulated the opening and closing of its stomata. When it was especially hot and dry, our magnolia was in danger. Warmer and dryer air increases the amount of evaporation. Dryer soil decreases the amount of water available for absorption. Together, they significantly diminish the amount of water available to the plant, which diminishes the plant's ability to photosynthesize, and reduces cell turgor in leaves, making them wilt, making them poor receptors of sunlight.

Transpiration is not all bad. It is essential for the long-distance transport of water from roots to shoots and leaves. Plants transpire impressive amounts of water. A large oak weighs about 13,600 kilograms. On an average summer day, it can transpire about 378.5 liters of water, or 378.5 kilograms. Thus, in a single day, it sheds a quantity of water equal to 2.78% of its total weight. Now think about the energy required to 'lift' that much weight from roots to leaves. Does xylem constrict from root to apex, pumping water upwards? No. Instead, most botanists believe that water moves upwards from the roots due to water's tendency to cohere together and to adhere to other materials. Strange though it might be, water is sticky. As it evaporates in the upper parts of the plant, water molecules are pulled upward by cohesion.

Day after day, month after month, year after year, our magnolia did these things.

Representative of the majority of plants (the vascular, seed-bearing, flowering plants), our magnolia, throughout its life, has actively maintained itself in the face of changing and dangerous conditions. The majority of plants thus fit Enactivism's conception of mindedness.

Like the case against plant minds, the case for plant minds can be tidily summarized:

1 Autopoiesis-and-adaptivity suffice for having a mind.
2 Plants are autopoietic-and-adaptive.
3 So, plants have minds.

Most contemporary philosophers of mind and cognitive scientists will reject Premise 1. As we have seen in this section (and starting back in Chapter Three), the main argument for accepting Premise 1 is that to have a mind is to have or create a world of things with meaning for oneself, and autopoiesis-and-adaptivity suffice for exactly that. Even if that is modestly compelling, many theorists will still reject Premise 1, for it has a wildly implausible consequence. It implies that every living thing has a mind.

Thus, an adequate defense of the idea that plants have minds must address this apparent problem.

4. Against and for Mind in Life

I admit: the idea that all living thing have a mind seems outlandish. It means that even bacteria—though probably not viruses—have minds.[7] If that's right, since I am host to billions of bacteria, Walt Whitman was right in a way that he didn't envision: "I contain multitudes." I am filled with many minds.

For ease of reference, and in acknowledgement of Evan Thompson's book, let us give a label to the claim that all living things have a mind; call it the "Mind in Life Thesis." That thesis differs from what Peter Godfrey-Smith calls the "Weak Continuity Thesis": Anything with a mind is alive. Mind in Life does not imply and is not implied by Weak Continuity. (In general, the claim that all A's are B's does not imply that all B's are A's.)[8]

If asked, probably very many contemporary cognitive scientists and many philosophers of mind would accept Weak Continuity.[9] It is curious, then, that contemporary theorizing about the mind is 'lifeless.' Only very few theorists have explored why or whether Weak Continuity is true. Why is it that, as far we know, only living things have minds? Perhaps it is a mere contingency or 'accident,' and there really are—or, anyway, could be—things with minds that are not alive. If so, it would be very nice to know why. My point here is only that theorists should be more interested in the connection between mind and life than they seem to be. They should be interested in Weak Continuity, as well as its seemingly strange converse, Mind in Life.

Why does Mind in Life strike us as strange? Does its strangeness just reflect our prejudices? It might seem just obvious that not all living things have minds, but it's not exactly easy to explain why that cannot be. Surely there isn't a law of nature forbidding it.

To support the Mind in Life Thesis, I will present several objections that one might make against it, offering a reply to each.[10]

1. *Dumb Life*. Autopoiesis—which allegedly suffices for being alive—does not suffice for having a mind. Producing and maintaining a 'self'—and talk of a 'self' here is seriously misleading—does not involve any of the hallmarks of a mind, such as perceiving, feeling, remembering, or voluntary action. We can grant that the maintenance performed by cells, and by aggregates of cells in larger organisms, is sophisticated and impressive. Of course life is impressive! But creating organelles, keeping them segregated from an environment, manufacturing or acquiring energy, and expelling toxic byproducts does not require any comprehension or understanding of what is happening or that anything at all is happening. Self-producing things can be totally clueless. To claim that 'self'-production (and adaptivity) suffices for having a mind is to stretch the concept of mind beyond recognition.

Reply to Dumb Life. It is not a stretch to think that self-production and adaptivity suffice for mind. Many respectable contemporary philosophers actually claim that science—an esteemed pinnacle of intelligence—is rational precisely because it is (at its best) 'self-correcting.' Scientists are fallible: they have limited resources, equipment, time, and energy; they misinterpret results; they fail to perform experiments; they overlook questions; they can be biased and petty. These facts can make you worry that science is not rational. But influential philosophers such as Karl Popper, Wilfrid Sellars, and Bas van Fraassen say that science is rational, when it is rational, not because it is infallible but because it corrects its mistakes.[11] *Good* science reinterprets data, pursues unperformed experiments, asks unasked questions, rejects beliefs exposed as false, and so on. Self-correction was at work when we recognized that the sun does not go around the earth, and that many diseases are transmissible by germs. This is, of course, different from and more sophisticated than the self-production and maintenance that we see in bacteria and plants. But they are substantively similar. Crucially, since we readily acknowledge that the self-correcting character of science helps qualify science as intelligent, we can acknowledge that autopoietic systems are intelligent or have a mind, without unduly stretching our concept of mind.

2. *Deceptive Appearance.* Mind in Life is dangerously close to endorsing the Argument from Design, which Darwin showed us was mistaken. The Argument from Design says that living things must have a designer because they are so incredibly well suited to their circumstances, they appear to be designed. However, evolution by natural selection, in which successive generations develop finely different traits, is a compelling alternative explanation. Tantalizing though it might be, we must resist the urge to think that because living things *seem* intelligent, they *really are* intelligent. There is a perfectly good alternative explanation for that appearance: Living things are well adapted to their circumstances due to evolution by natural selection. Mind in Life confuses the long-wrought effects of evolution with having a mind.

Reply to Deceptive Appearance. For all Darwin did, organisms still seem intelligent. That is easily overlooked. Explaining how things could *appear* to be designed without a designer—undermining the Argument from Design—does nothing at all to erase that appearance. Just set this book down, step outside, and have a look around. Nature is astonishing, not just for its diversity or beauty, but also for the way in which things weirdly 'work.' Think about everything that we have discussed here in this book. Run your mind's time-lapse video of shoots bending toward the sun, or of roots bending to avoid pebbles in the soil. Organisms appear *intelligent*, remarkably responsive to their changing circumstances. The fact that organisms evolved should not compel us to say that they *only appear* intelligent, but *aren't really* so. Instead, we should remember that intelligent things can result from evolution. We regard ourselves as the paradigm of intelligence, and we resulted from evolution. Accepting that organisms evolved is perfectly consistent with accepting that they are also intelligent.

3. *Denying Differences.* We should acknowledge the deep similarities between all living things, but Mind in Life obliterates real differences that we should keep separate. Living things grow, seek energy, metabolize, and reproduce. They self-maintain. These abilities are not the same as having a mind—perceiving, feeling, remembering, and acting. *Some* living things have minds and are intelligent, but *not all*. (Compare: *Some* animals are mammals, but *not all*.) True, everything with a mind that we know of is alive, but that does not imply that all living things have a mind. (Compare: All mammals are animals, but not all animals are mammals.) Growing, seeking energy, metabolizing, and reproducing show no comprehension, no capacity to appreciate the implications of such activity, of what would be a good reason for or against such activity, no grasp of what one is reacting to or why. Consider how some bacteria are drawn to sugar. Being so drawn is only a meager prelude to genuinely perceiving sugar. Sensing and perceiving differ not in degree, but in kind. Perception of sugar can be accurate or inaccurate—as a picture or a chemist's report can be. Mere sensing of sugar can be neither; it is mere responsiveness to sugar—as when water adheres to salt. Perception characterizes a target as being some way or other. Mere sensing does not; it is a mere reaction to something. Continuity encourages us to ignore that difference.

Reply to Denying Differences. We can acknowledge that all organisms are intelligent or have minds without ignoring important differences between them. Insisting otherwise is like complaining that squares shouldn't be classified as polygons because some other polygons have traits very different from squares. Calling squares 'polygons,' and grouping them together with triangles, trapezoids, and octagons, doesn't obliterate the differences between them. Doing so draws attention to striking similarities. Polygons are two-dimensional, many-sided, closed figures. They differ from curved, closed figures (such as circles) and three-dimensional, many-sided, closed figures (such as pyramids). Calling plants and bacteria 'intelligent' or saying they have proto-minds and placing them on a spectrum with dogs and humans doesn't obliterate the differences between them. It draws attention to interesting similarities: they all take care of themselves in changing environments that threaten their existence. Saying that all organisms are organisms, or that they all are alive, also doesn't obliterate differences between them. In our languages, we have more- and less-specific terms, each with its role. Sometimes we need to group many things together; sometimes we need to separate things from one another. Sometimes we want to talk about granite specifically, and not all rocks. Sometimes we want to talk about all dogs, not just Labradors. And sometimes we want to talk about intelligent things, not just the ones that perceive, or have episodic memory, or language. We should not banish all generic terms in favor of maximally specific ones. Doing so would preclude us from discussing real similarities.

4. *Romantic Fantasy*. Mind in Life expresses an excessively romantic, even fantastic way of thinking in which all organisms are somehow unified beyond merely being alive. In one ancient version of this idea, nature is a single, conscious entity, somehow overseeing its own super-life. Gaia was the ancient Greek goddess of the Earth. The idea of such an entity persists in talk of Mother Nature. In the 1970s, James Lovelock and Lynn Margulis articulated the "Gaia hypothesis," the idea that the entire bio-sphere of the Earth is not just a collection of organisms but a single system. That has come to be a reputable idea. Some even contend further that it is a single organism.[12] Who knows why some of us are drawn to such an idea? Perhaps it makes our existence seem more meaningful or less pointless. Perhaps it is a symptom of unconscious guilt about our appallingly arrogant mistreatment of nonhuman nature. Whatever its source, it is mistaken. Although Mind in Life may provide some temporary respite, we have other good ways to deal with our fears and failures.

Reply to Romantic Fantasy. As we have seen, there are reasons to accept Mind in Life that have nothing to do with fantastic, romantic yearnings to be one with all of nature. Enactivism, which is one way of clarifying Mind in Life, proposes that self-production and active adjustment in response to better and worse environmental circumstances suffices for having a mind—for disclosing a world of things that have significance. (It is compatible with the claim that human minds, which perceive, feel, remember, and act voluntarily, require more.) Far from being an expression of naïve, antiquated mysticism, Mind in Life is supported by our best, most current understanding of mind *and life*. It is one more step past Descartes's Dualism, which—you will remember—held that minds and bodies are fundamentally different sorts of things. Furthermore, it is also a step past the Computational Theory of Mind, which ignores the actual material details of real minds, focusing solely on some of their (admittedly important) organizational properties, never stopping to acknowledge that so far as we know, only living things have minds.

Enactivism says that all living things are autopoietic systems, and that such systems have at least a minimal form of mind. For they disclose (or 'enact') an environment, an 'umwelt,' an array of things with significance. They create and inhabit a field of opportunities and threats, things that matter to them in various ways, things that they should or should not do. By avoiding threats and pursuing opportunities, they maintain their selves, maintaining the border between self and non-self.

Think about things with minds, like us. I clearly inhabit an 'umwelt,' a field of things that have significance. Things 'show up' to me as mattering in some way or other. That contributes to me having a point of view. I am drawn to that coffee on my desk; I flinch as a wasp buzzes through my window; my ears prick up at the sound of kettle drums. I keep myself going by engaging in various ways with these things. My milieu might be larger, more variegated, and complexly interwoven than that of bacteria and plants, for I have an imagination, and am capable of abstract thought. Things in my environments are not easily classed simply into 'threats' and 'opportunities.' But none of that implies that plants or bacteria also don't have an umwelt, fields of things that have significance for them.

Furthermore, our activities 'enact' or disclose the world, and the difference between we who have a perspective and that on which a perspective is had, a field of things that matter. I am not talking about creating a *physical* border, a membrane. I am not talking about skin care. I am talking about the more ethereal difference between you and that which matters to you. Your activities—your pursuit and avoidance of things—are essential to your very existence, to there being a *you* and a field of things that matter to you. I am not talking about *which things* matter to *you* (cups of coffee, or wasps), or *the ways* in which they matter (as offering a refreshing taste, or as a danger to your body). I am talking about there being a field of things that matter *at all*. If you were to cease pursuing or avoiding things entirely, there would cease to be a field of things that matter, and thereby you, too, would cease to be. If nothing at all mattered to you—not friendship or petty rivalries, not coffee or wasps—you would waste away. Your body might continue to function in some minimal sense, but you would be gone.

This is not a romantic fantasy, but a valuable insight that many intelligent biologists, psychologists, and philosophers have missed. It presses us to consider or reconsider what we think of living things, to better understand how they are similar and different.

5. *Impractical*. Mind in Life encourages us to be foolishly protective of all organisms. Since we should avoid unnecessarily harming anything that has a mind, we would have to avoid unnecessarily harming *every* organism—plants, fungi, and bacteria included. That would paralyze humanity. For us to live, at least some organisms must die. We are not autotrophs: We cannot endogenously manufacture our own energy, but must get it from elsewhere, either from organisms that do, or from organisms that get it from them. Other living things are not just our food. They also become our clothes, shelter, and medicine. Accepting Mind in Life would force us to alter significantly our use of other living things.

Reply to Impractical. If we accept Mind in Life, it isn't clear exactly how we would need to change our ways. We could acknowledge that all organisms have proto-minds without feeling obliged to be more protective of them. In discussions of animal welfare, for instance, their capacity to suffer pain is a main reason for being protective of them, for insisting on 'animal rights.' It's not clear that plants or bacteria feel pain, at all.

Still, we would do well to reconsider the sorts of thing that surround us, fill us, and upon which we depend. I myself find it oddly easy to forget that I am alive, that plants are alive, that I am filled with fully living colonies of bacteria. If Mind in Life is true, we are immersed in intelligence. That doesn't mean that everything happens for a reason. Nor is it an invitation to let nature run its course, as if nature were some all-knowing, all-good steward that can be left alone without anyone to critically reflect on it. Rather, it is to acknowledge that our conscious minds—what we sometimes lazily slide into thinking of when we think of intelligence—are far from the only intelligent thing around. We are not surrounded by, filled with, and made of simply dumb matter that aimlessly bumps around, but elaborate networks of autopoietic systems. We humans thus turn out to be both smarter and dumber than we often think we are. Our human bodies do sophisticated things that we don't normally notice, and which we don't or can't consciously or unconsciously control. And nonhuman organisms are more sophisticated, more intelligent, closer to us than we commonly admit.

Whether or not we accept Mind in Life, diligent research and activism have shown us that for our own sake, we need to seriously improve how we deal with nonhuman animals, plants, and bacteria. Some worthy improvements are clearer than others. As just one example, we should resist monocultures, farming practices that drastically reduce the diversity of varieties of a species (such as wheat) in preference for one single variety, which is actively cultivated to dominate all suitable habitats. It is exceedingly simplistic to think that Mind in Life forces us merely to be 'more protective.'

5. Self-correction

By raising and responding to a variety of objections, I have just tried to persuade you that Mind in Life is not outlandish, but plausible. If I have succeeded, Enactivism and plant minds should also look more plausible than they previously did. In turn, we can reject the Computational Theory of Mind, its claim that minds require representations, and the attendant implication that plants don't have minds. However, if I haven't succeeded, and

Mind in Life still looks outlandish to you, then so, too, will Enactivism, and we are left without a case in favor of plant minds.

At the start of this book, I admitted that the idea of plant minds initially seemed silly to me. Although I knew very little about plants, I did know a good bit about theories of minds, and for me it was beyond question that plants don't have minds.

Having now looked more closely, I have changed my mind. Plants are vastly more sophisticated than I realized, and our concepts of mind and intelligence are more flexible than I used to think. No longer do I think the idea of plant minds is silly. By highlighting the connection between autopoiesis-and-adaptivity and the 'disclosure' of an umwelt, a world of meaning, more than mere space, Enactivism makes it plausible that plants and other organisms have minds. This is a substantial and welcome advance beyond what should be regarded as a thoughtless dogma in mainstream cognitive science and mainstream ('Western') philosophy of mind, the idea that mind has nothing to do with life, as if it is just an inexplicable and uninteresting accident that only living things have minds.

Correcting myself—my former confidently held belief that plants definitely don't have minds—is a fitting way to recognize my continuity with the self-correcting behavior of plants.

Notes

1 See, especially, (Dewey, 1925/2000) and (Heidegger, 1927/1962).
2 See, especially, Dreyfus' *What Computers (Still) Can't Do*, and Haugeland's *Artificial Intelligence*. See also (Haugeland, 1978), (Haugeland, 1979), and (Haugeland, 1995), collected in (Haugeland, 1998).
3 More recently, these ideas have been championed by Andy Clark, e.g., (Clark, 1997).
4 (van Gelder, 1995). For further elaboration, see (van Gelder, 1998). Three decades earlier, Hans Jonas also discussed Watt's governor as important to a properly philosophical biology (Jonas, 1966).
5 One could, of course, *say* that the angle of the arms represents the speed of the engine, but doing so is gratuitous. Nothing is gained by doing so; such talk doesn't help us understand the governor any better.
6 (Schuman, Barthel, & Baldwin, 2012).
7 Traditionally, viruses are not counted among the living. The main reason is that they cannot reproduce without commandeering the reproductive capacity of another entity. They also do not consume energy or excrete waste. For a good accessible discussion, see (Villareal, 2004).
8 Godfrey-Smith identifies another related thesis, which he labels "Strong Continuity": "Life and mind have a strong common abstract pattern or set of basic organizational properties. The functional properties characteristic of mind are an enriched version of the functional properties that are fundamental to life in general. Mind is literally life-*like*." Godfrey-Smith holds that Strong Continuity

128   *Mind in Life*

implies Weak Continuity, for it suggests an explanation for Weak Continuity. The Mind in Life Thesis does not imply and is not implied by Strong Continuity.

9 A main reason for rejecting it is the prospect of artificial intelligence—computers or robots with minds. But maybe any computer or robot that is 'sophisticated' enough to qualify as having a mind should qualify as being alive, even if it is not made from 'organic' molecules.

10 In his *Summa Theologica*, composed over nine years, but left unfinished at his death in 1274, Thomas Aquinas addresses a vast array of questions, relying on a distinctive technique to further his claims. For each question, instead of simply giving his answer and offering reasons for it, he starts with a series of answers opposed to his own, what he labels as "Objections." He then gives his own answer, and makes his case in part by replying to the opposed answers. That can be confusing, since Aquinas can seem to be contradicting what he previously said. But his strategy is remarkably powerful, for he earns your trust by admitting and giving priority to ideas that oppose his own, and then systematically explains why he doesn't accept those opposing ideas. That is what I do here: First I present a reason to reject Mind in Life, and then I explain why we can reject that reason.

11 (Popper, 1963/2002); (Sellars, 1956) reprinted in (deVries & Triplett, 2000); and (van Fraassen, 1980).

12 (Lovelock, 1972) and (Lovelock & Margulis, 1974).

Works Cited

Clark, A. (1997). *Being There: Putting Brain, Body and World Together Again.* Cambridge, MA: MIT Press.

deVries, W., & Triplett, T. (2000). *Knowledge, Mind and the Given.* New York: Hackett.

Dewey, J. (1925/2000). *Experience and Nature.* Mineola, NY: Dover.

Haugeland, J. (1978). The Nature and Plausibility of Cognitivism. *Behavioral and Brain Sciences, 1*(2), 215–226.

Haugeland, J. (1979). Understanding Natural Language. *Journal of Philosophy, 76*(11), 619–632.

Haugeland, J. (1995). Mind Embodied and Embedded (L. Haaparanta & S. Heinämaa, Eds.). *Acta Philosophica Fennica, 58*, 233–267.

Haugeland, J. (1998). *Having Thought.* Cambridge, MA: Harvard University Press.

Heidegger, M. (1927/1962). *Being and Time* (J. Macquarrie & E. Robinson, Trans.). New York: Harper.

Jonas, H. (1966). *The Phenomenon of Life: Toward a Philosophical Biology.* New York: Harper & Row.

Lovelock, J. (1972). Gaia as Seen Through the Atmosphere. *Atmospheric Environment, 6*(8), 579–580.

Lovelock, J., & Margulis, L. (1974). Atmospheric Homeostasis by and for the Biosphere: The Gaia Hypothesis. *Tellus, 26*(1–2), 2–10.

Popper, K. (1963/2002). Science: Conjectures and Refutations. In K. Popper (Ed.), *Conjectures and Refutations* (pp. 43–77). New York: Routledge.

Schuman, M., Barthel, K., & Baldwin, I. (2012, October 15). Herbivory-Induced Volatiles Function as Defenses Increasing Fitness of the Native Plant Nicotiana attenuata in Nature. *eLife* 2012;1:e00007

Sellars, W. (1956). Empiricism and the Philosophy of Mind. In H. Feigl, M. Scriven, & G. Maxwell (Eds.), *Minnesota Studies in the Philosophy of Science* (Vol. 1, pp. 253–329). Minneapolis: University of Minnesota Press.

van Fraassen, B. (1980). *The Scientific Image*. New York: Clarendon.

van Gelder, T. (1995). What Might Cognition Be, If Not Computation? *The Journal of Philosophy, 92*(7), 345–381.

van Gelder, T. (1998). The Dynamical Hypothesis in Cognitive Science (With Commentary and Replies). *Behavioral and Brain Sciences, 21*(5), 615–665.

Villareal, L. (2004, December). Are Viruses Alive? *Scientific American*, 101–105.

Index

action *see* movement; tropisms
adaptation 108
adaptive 71–3, 115
adaptivity 76n47, 120–2, 127
Aquinas, Saint Thomas 7, 23n10, 25n56, 128n10
Aristotle 4–5, 7, 9, 15, 23n7, 38, 42, 50n23, 106
autopoiesis 71–3, 76n47, 115, 121–3, 125, 127
auxin 39, 41, 61, 74n17, 87, 90, 108

bacteria 32–3, 42, 50n7, 62, 72, 93, 116, 118, 121, 123–7
behaviorism 13–19, 21, 109n9; Radical 16–19, 21, 24nn43–4, 101–2
Boysen-Jensen experiments 38–9

Calvo, P. 23n3, 25n55, 25n59, 75n20, 75n40, 84, 95nn1–2, 95n11
Cartesian Dualism 8–9, 12, 15, 21, 124
Chalmers, D. 63–4, 75n26, 75n28
Chamowitz, D. 30, 84, 87, 95n1, 95nn3–4, 95n10, 98
chemomorphism 100, 106
Computational Theory of Mind (Computationalism; Computational-Representational Theory of Mind) 18–21, 102, 105–6, 114–15, 124, 126
computer 19–20, 25n56, 103–5, 107–8, 109n10, 128n9; *see also* formal system
conditioning 82–3, 101
consciousness 15–16, 57, 64, 67, 69, 73, 74n8, 74n10, 75n31, 76n47, 101
constancy 48–9

Continuity Thesis: Strong 127n8; Weak 121
Cummins, R. 89, 96n17, 96n19

Darwin, C. 4, 10–13, 15, 24nn30–1, 31, 38–9, 50n5, 61, 74n3, 75n19, 89, 122
Darwin, F. 15, 24n31, 24n39, 38–9, 50n5, 61, 74n3, 75n19
Dennett, D. 107–8, 109n12, 109nn19–20
Descartes, R. 7–9, 21, 23n9, 24n16–20, 24n23, 58
Dewey, J. 113–14, 127n1
disclosing 70, 72, 115, 124–7; *see also* matter
dogs 13–14, 16, 47–8, 51n33, 82, 101–2, 106
domains (of life) 32
Dretske, F. 25n59, 50n2, 96n23, 109n14, 109n18
Dreyfus, H. 25n57, 114, 127n2

Enactivism 69–73, 114, 120, 124, 126
eukaryotes 32–3
evolution 10–12, 32–3, 36, 89, 91–2, 122–3
explanatory gap 63, 67

feedback loops 94–5, 96n27, 98
finches 11
flowers 35–6
formal system 103–4; automatic 104; interpreted 104
Frisch, K. von 102, 109n8
fruit flies 82–3
function 88; Systemic View 90; Etiological View 91–2

Printed in the United States
by Baker & Taylor Publisher Services